MW00913054

What readers are saying:

"Both memoir and travelogue, Still Life with Sierra follows one family's journey through the continents of grief, anger, fear, and love. I want to send copies to all my friends who are dealing with losses of their own."

Sheri Reynolds, author of The Rapture of Canaan, a New York Times bestseller, and The Sweet In-Between and professor of creative writing at Old Dominion University

"The loss of a child would seem to be inexpressible, but Peggy Sijswerda conveys her bereavement—and difficult journey back from it—with an eloquent candor that transcends sadness. That eventful journey takes her family great distances, geographically and emotionally. Ultimately, intimately, the writer brings all of us back home."

Bill Ruehlmann, columnist, author, and professor of journalism at Virginia Wesleyan College

"Peggy Sijswerda shares in vivid, poignant detail the journey she and her family traveled following the tragic drowning death of her two-year-old daughter. Still Life with Sierra is unusual because of the visceral insights we gain into the author's soul as she attempts to make sense of 'a sorrow beyond tears.' We learn rare truths about the twists and rewards buried in the slow process of healing. A worthy read."

Virginia O'Keefe, freelance writer and author of Speaking to Think/Thinking to Speak

"A remarkable story of a family's journey to healing after the accidental death of a child. The emotional honesty in this unique book gives permission to our truest forms of grieving and shows how diverse our paths of recovery from grief must always be. I would highly recommend it to anyone who has struggled with unbearable loss."

Lindsay C. Gibson, Psy.D., clinical psychologist and author of Who You Were Meant to Be: A Guide to Finding or Rediscovering Your Life's Purpose

Sierra M. Sijswerda

VIRGINIA BEACH — Sierra Margriet Sijswerda, 3, of the 2700 block of Atwoodtown Road, died Aug. 18, 1990.

Sierra was a native of Virginia Beach.

Survivors include her parents, Peggy and Peter Sijswerda, and two brothers, Scott Sijswerda and Jasper Sijswerda, all of Virginia Beach; maternal grandmother, Phyllis Heberling of Virginia Beach; maternal grandfather, Donald A. Heberling of Oklawaha, Fla.; and paternal grandparents, Mr. and Mrs. Pieter Sijswerda of the Netherlands.

A memorial service will be conducted at 11 a.m. Wednesday in Sandbridge Community United Methodist Chapel by the Rev. Ed Martin. Burial will be private. Friends may join the family from 6 to 8 p.m. today at 2753 Atwoodtown Road. H.D. Oliver Funeral Apartments, Laskin Road, is handling arrangements.

Memorial donations may be made to Hospice Care Inc., 204 27th St., Suite D, Virginia Beach, Va. 23451.

—⟨∿⟩—

Still
Life with
Sierra

by Peggy Sijswerda

—⟨∿⟩—

Windmill Promotions, Inc.
Virginia Beach, Virginia

Copyright © 2010

All rights reserved. No part of this book may be reproduced in any form or by any electronic or mechanical means, including information storage and retrieval systems, without
permission in writing from the author, except by a reviewer who may quote brief passages
in a review.

Printed in the United States of America.

Windmill Promotions, Inc.
3065 Mansfield Lane
Virginia Beach, VA 23457

Visit www.peggysijswerda.com or email sijswerda@hotmail.com for further information.

Acknowledgments

—◦◦◦—

In gratitude

I have come to believe that every person who crosses our paths in life has something to teach us. We need only to figure out what it is. Since Sierra died twenty years ago, my path has intersected with those of numerous people—friends and strangers—each of whom was a stepping stone toward this moment.

I want to thank my professors in Old Dominion University's creative writing program, especially Michael Pearson; Virginia O'Keefe, whose editor's eye helped polish my story; my many friends who have helped me gain courage and strength, especially in the darker days; my brothers, who know how much they mean to me; my mother, whose cheerful smile never fails to brighten my day; my sons, whose hugs and mischievous ways ground me when I most need it; and my husband, Peter, whose love and support make each day better than the last.

I dedicate this book to the memories of Sierra Margriet Sijswerda, 1987-1990, my little Dutch girl, and to my father, Donald Anthony Heberling, USN, Ret., 1923-2003, who taught me to love life.

Foreword

———✎✎✎———

Wisps of smoke

Writing a memoir necessitates reporting on and interpreting to some extent the thoughts and feelings of others. As such, the memoirist sees people and events through a lens, one that both colors memories and lends a soft focus to things that were once sharp-edged. In writing this memoir, I strove for accuracy and credibility while reporting on my family's feelings and actions at the time of Sierra's death and during the ensuing years.

Fortunately, I was able to corroborate events and conversations with my husband, Peter, whose help in writing this story has proven invaluable. I also relied on journals which I kept during the more intense periods depicted in this memoir; these provided invaluable insight into my own thoughts and feelings as I wandered sometimes blindly along my journey.

My older sons also kept journals during our travels, and their comments and pictures evoke memories which otherwise, like wisps of smoke, would have dissipated with time. Photos and videos, especially during our year abroad, also lent authority to the memoir. Conversations were recreated from memory and therefore reflect the essence of what was said rather than the exact words used.

Characters drive memoir, and painting my family and those I met on my journey in vivid colors with subtle shades of detail and nuance requires a certain insight into the fundamentals of personality. While I can't claim to see inside the minds and motivations of the people I painted in this memoir, I can offer my own interpretation, just as an artist does.

Introduction

—∽∾∽—

The story of the story

The story you are holding is alive. Every day it grows bigger. In the beginning I hoped it would go away, but this story refused to be ignored. It elbowed its way into my consciousness, often with sharp jabs that brought hot tears to my eyes. For many years I worked harder at not telling the story than telling it. But this story has patience and wisdom. It knew it could wait.

In time I discovered this story needed to be told and, finally, that I needed to tell it. But the route to the telling has been circuitous. I'm not even sure whether the story is finished with me. I am bound up in this story so deeply that I cannot tell anymore where the story ends and I begin. We are joined like the horizon to the sea on those misty days when you can't tell where the water ends and the sky begins. They mingle like dancers over a watery grave.

Because this story lives, it changes shape and meaning often. Like an amoeba, it shifts and wiggles and wanders where it wants. I try to follow it, to keep up. Sometimes I want to say, "Wait! Whose story is this? Why can't I just tell it and be done with it?"

A distant trill of laughter responds, a happy sound, and I want to follow it.

ii.

I can't remember when I decided I wanted to write. No one ever suggested I become a writer, although in high school and college, teachers complimented me on my skill with words. Perhaps no one encouraged me to pursue writing as a career because making a living as a writer is hard. Writing, like art, is a vocation for people who have money or who don't mind doing without the luxuries in life.

Instead I chose a career as an English teacher, and life in general was fulfilling for many years. Then my world changed in a moment, and being fulfilled stopped mattering so much.

Sometime during the haze that followed, a small voice inside began to whisper, "You have something to say."

"What?" I asked.

"Ponder," the voice answered.

So I pondered. Then I began to write. I enrolled in a feature writing class in 1994, and our professor encouraged us to try creative nonfiction. I wasn't sure exactly what that was, but I read the examples and decided the idea of creative nonfiction—using literary elements, such as setting, dialogue, theme, and descriptive writing, to tell true stories that speak about the human condition—appealed to me. I gave it a try.

I wrote about Compassionate Friends, a bereavement support group my husband, Peter, and I attended after our daughter, Sierra, died. I handed in the paper unfinished. My teacher said the writing moved him. He encouraged me to finish the piece. I couldn't. I didn't even try. I knew I wasn't ready. The story wasn't ready, either. It needed to grow.

iii.

Writing about things that hurt isn't easy, but it helps you figure them out. When you write, it's as if you free your subconscious mind so it can take you where you need to go. Writing is a process of discovery. Like a treasure hunt, you pick up clues along the way, each one leading to the next. As you get closer to the treasure at the end, you pick up speed, and soon you're running to find the next clue. I discovered that if you run too fast, you'll miss things. It's better to take your time, stop and rest along the way, close your eyes, and inhale the smells around you. Breathe. Think about how lucky you are to be alive.

Often if you turn around and look, you'll find clues right behind you. As the story of Sierra began to take shape in my mind, I needed to go backwards, to board a plane and fly across the years, scanning the landscape of my life for clues about how to make sense of the present. I found that the shadows of the past are long. They are attached to us, to our feet. You can't walk away from them. You have to make friends with the shadows of your past.

In the spring of 1997, I enrolled in a creative nonfiction class at Old Dominion University. After learning more about the genre by reading classic works of nonfiction, we began writing. I chose to write a travel piece about the summer of 1982 when I'd gone abroad with my mother. As hard as I tried to make it meaningful, the piece remained flat. The paper ended when a handsome waiter named Peter first served me breakfast in an Amsterdam hotel. That waiter would one day become my husband.

"This is where the story should begin," my instructor said. But that wasn't the story that simmered inside me. It was a part of the story, an important piece. And while it would take a few more years before the pieces would begin to fit together, this first attempt was a required step. It was almost as if I were accruing the necessary skills to apply for a new job. Writing the story of Sierra was becoming my new occupation—only I didn't know it yet.

iv.

When someone dies, it's natural to think about what matters in life. It's a question worth pondering because once you know the answer, so many things fall into place. Too often we think the things that matter are tangible, like houses, cars, high-definition television. I've learned the hard way that the tangible things that matter breathe and grow. When my son Ross hugs me, that matters. He's fifteen now, and sometimes he almost knocks me over with his enthusiastic hugs. I'm not sure how Ross ended up being so affectionate, but I am forever grateful for it. He blows kisses when he leaves the house. He still wants an occasional snuggle at night. He tells me he loves me every time we talk on the phone.

If my daughter hadn't died, Ross might not even be here.

Some people say our children are never ours. We borrow them from the universe for a while. Some say children who die young came to us for a special reason. It's up to us to figure out what that reason is.

The first time I tried to tell the story of Sierra was during a second creative nonfiction workshop I took in the fall of 1999. By now I had decided to enter the MFA program at ODU, a six-year journey that would take me zigzagging through a varied landscape, sometimes barren and full of rocks, other times lush and green with new growth.

That fall I wrote a piece telling about my family's recent move to Europe. In it I mentioned Sierra's death briefly—as if it weren't important, just an aside.

My classmates, shocked by the revelation, wanted to know more about Sierra's death. I responded, "But this isn't about her."

I would come to find out that, in fact, it was all about her. Not just the story I was writing, not just the move abroad that the story detailed, but the shape of my life, the pattern it created. It was as if the story of Sierra were my opponent in a chess game, each side trying to outwit the other, trying to win.

v.

Telling the story of Sierra meant looking deep inside myself. Most people tend to go through life without getting to know themselves very well. In fact, we surround ourselves with so many distractions that we never find time to reflect.

Noise is one distraction that permeates modern life. Think for a moment about the noises you're hearing right now. If you're lucky, you might hear the wind blowing through the trees or frogs croaking, but if a television drones in the background, I suggest you get up and turn it off. Now stop reading and listen to the silence. You might even want to close your eyes and open your mind to whatever thoughts may come. If none do, that's OK. Keep reading, but in the days ahead, remember to find a silent place where you can be alone. Learning to become comfortable with yourself in a quiet space is important in life's journey.

As I dove deeper into the story of Sierra, I needed to go deeper into myself. Learning what her life meant to me required first discovering what my life meant. Sierra's path and mine have intersected at times, collided at others, but always there is movement toward something.

In 1999 I started a regional magazine for women called *Tidewater Women*. Learning more about myself became a priority. I also knew this magazine could help other women on their journey toward fulfillment. So many women neglect their own needs while carrying out their roles as wives, mothers, and daughters. *Tidewater Women* could help them, I decided, through inspiring, informative editorial. I also knew the process of shaping the magazine would help me learn and grow.

Examining our lives brings understanding. While some call this process navel gazing, I believe the more questions we ask, the more we know. Besides, what's the alternative? Staring at the television night after night or, worse, into the bottom of your empty Scotch on the rocks? I wanted more from life.

Drawn to explore the mind-body-spirit relationship, I decided to begin with massage. A therapist named Barbara had contacted me about advertising, and I decided to experience a massage with her. I showed up for my appointment and found Barbara to be a warm, kind woman. We talked a bit, and I learned her husband had died two years before. After his death she had moved from the Northeast with her daughter to start over in Virginia Beach with a new career as a massage therapist.

I wasn't ready to tell Barbara about Sierra, but I was struck by the irony that the universe had brought us together. Barbara was on a journey of self-discovery, too. When her husband died, the foundation of her life caved in, yet here she was bravely, somewhat gingerly making her way forward, moving toward something, maybe she didn't know just what.

I'd only experienced a professional massage once before, and while the bodywork had been satisfactory, there had been no spiritual connection. Barbara, on the other hand, explained that her massage therapy involved a spiritual component and began with a prayer. As I lay on the massage table, hearing the birds twittering outside and the meditative music playing softly, Barbara began to speak in a hushed voice, asking for assistance as she prepared to perform her massage. She also asked me to open up my mind, to let the universe do its work. She instructed me to relax and breathe deeply.

What came next was an incredible journey into relaxation. My mind entered a realm it hardly knew, a place where secrets live, where primordial desires and dreams dwell. While Barbara massaged my body, I sank into this netherworld, a space suspended between this moment and all the other moments that exist. Near the end, Barbara, who had spoken very little, asked what she thought was an innocent question.

"Do you have any children?"

The tears came as quickly as if I had been cut with a knife. I couldn't even answer her at first. I tried to say, "I have three sons," but I couldn't speak. Barbara remained silent while I struggled to control my emotions. Then I told her about Sierra. Afterwards I felt emotionally drained, but sensed energy flowing through my body. I knew that there were still many miles ahead, but I felt as if I were going in the right direction at last.

vi.

P art of my MFA program required that I take three writing tutorials with visiting writers. In the fall of 2000, I worked with the first one, an award-winning theater critic and freelance writer from New York. This writer had a fast-talking, urban style that some considered abrasive, but since she was one of the first real writers I'd ever met, I bowed to her, anxious about whether she would like my work.

The visiting writer had recently edited a collection of memoirs, brutally honest stories about sex abuse, family trauma, and addictive behaviors. The stories were what she called "victim and shame narratives," glimpses into memoirists' dark, private worlds. As I read a few of them, I realized that through telling their tormented stories, these authors seemed to achieve catharsis.

Immediately this writer zeroed in on the story of Sierra.

"I think you should write about that day, Peggy," she said, a not-so-subtle challenge in her words. She knew it would be hard, so she gave me writing prompts: Write five sentences about what I liked about Sierra, then what I didn't like about Sierra, then five sentences describing what I liked about me, then five telling what I didn't like about me.

Those prompts got me going. I started to write about my daughter, taking baby steps down a path full of thickets, each one hiding a memory I was afraid to remember. But somehow I sensed I was finally ready to begin telling the story.

I began by writing about a framed print I have on my wall of a tall young woman with blonde hair the color of wheat fields at sunset, hair that just brushes her shoulders. She stands amid red poppies in a white dress with an empty straw basket in her hand. Two geese stand placidly by her side, but she doesn't seem aware of them. She looks far away, somewhere I can't see, as if she's searching for something. I liked the dreaminess of the print, the sense of promise it evoked.

Then I wrote about living with a broken promise and trying to fix it. I wrote about my cousin, Julie, who died a month before Sierra. I wrote about Sierra's barrettes: the plastic butterflies, poodles, lovebirds, violins, and daisies in pretty pastel shades. I wrote about how many things in my life broke the day Sierra died: me, my family, my trust in God, my sense of peace, my belief that the world was a good place. I wrote about how I didn't understand what happened. Finally I wrote about the day Sierra died.

When the writer and I met at Starbucks, I handed her my short paper and went to get coffee. I sat and sipped from my cup while she read. I looked out the window and waited. When she finished reading, I was surprised to see tears in her eyes. I knew then I couldn't turn back. Sierra's story needed to be told.

vii.

A few years ago I tried an introductory Reiki session. I was writing a story for *Tidewater Women* and felt that adding my personal experience would flesh out the article. Reiki is an ancient healing art from Japan, but forms of this therapy are found in the Bible and other cultures. In elementary terms, Reiki involves the energy that flows within our bodies. When we are ill, the energy has become clogged up somewhere, and Reiki helps the energy begin flowing again. To an outsider, it would appear that Reiki practitioners are simply fanning their clients with their hands, but there's more to it than that.

Even though I wasn't sick, Reiki could help my energy flow even better, the therapist explained. So I lay on the table in the dim room and closed my eyes while two women moved around me, their hands fluttering like birds' wings. As the gentle currents of air brushed over me, I relaxed and time slipped by.

Too soon the session ended, and the practitioners said I should sit in a chair and rest a bit before driving home. The room was peaceful, and for a few moments I watched others getting their treatments. I saw a young man with straw-colored dread locks stuffed into a large hat and decided to interview him for the story.

We sat in a small room behind a closed door, and I started to ask the young man questions. Because of my relaxed state, I found it hard to speak cogently and apologized to the young man. He shrugged and then began telling me an amazing story about his grandfather communicating with him from the grave, about predicting his grandmother's death, about concerns from his priest that he be careful with his "gift." He even played back a recorded message from his cell phone left by the priest that affirmed these tales he was telling me.

All of a sudden the young man began staring deep into my eyes, and he said, "Something is troubling you." While he had been telling his story, my thoughts had turned to Sierra, and somehow he seemed to sense it. I felt compelled to tell him about Sierra, how she died, and how much I wished I could find out that she was all right.

He said, "You can." Then he gave me a crystal and said I should go home and make a small altar. I should place the crystal on the altar, along with a candle and perhaps a few mementos or anything that made me feel peaceful. If I did this and waited at the altar, she would come.

As I got into my car, the whole episode seemed like a dream, but there on the seat next to me lay the crystal. When I got home, I put the crystal in my dresser.

I never made the altar. I wasn't ready.

viii.

One of my dear friends doesn't care much for travel. She prefers to hang around Virginia Beach, lunch with friends, get together with family, putter around the garden, walk in the park. My friend is grounded to the earth in many ways, which is why she doesn't feel the need to escape. She has found her home and takes pleasure in her surroundings.

As someone who is incessantly restless, I envy my friend. I can't sit still for long. Perhaps growing up in a military family has kept me from wanting to put down roots. I prefer to be on the move, either coming or going. Sometimes it seems I am running from something, that travel is a distraction designed to keep me occupied. And it does, too. I am always planning a trip somewhere.

Maybe the whole idea of home frightens me. Home implies a feeling of contentment, of being settled. Maybe I'm afraid to be content, afraid a meteor will come crashing through the ether and fall smack on top of me or someone I love.

I am afraid, very afraid.

I try to hide my fear, but I know it's there. I want to overcome it, but I don't know how.

So I continue my journey. Maybe Sierra's story is helping me find the way.

ix.

Another MFA requirement was to participate in a self-directed internship called Writers in Community. One of my programs involved leading a women's writing group. Meeting once a week for six weeks, the women and I explored our lives through memoir. The group was a mixture of young and old, skilled and unskilled, but every woman had a story to tell.

One woman in her sixties wrote about how, at age 45, she had finally met the man she'd always dreamed of. She described their yearlong courtship and a love that grew so strong, it seemed straight out of a fairytale. Then this perfect man had a heart attack beside her in bed on their wedding night and died. She had never written down this story and hardly anyone had ever heard it.

The other members of the group and I sat, stunned. We knew this soft-spoken woman had broken through a barrier she'd hidden behind for too long. I knew there was a lesson for me in her story. I knew that just telling a story can have vast consequences.

That same spring I worked with another visiting author. She was a successful writer and psychotherapist. In fact, some of her books dealt with the themes of loss and recovery. I shared the pieces I had written for the New York writer, and she encouraged me to go deeper, further on my quest for understanding. I told her about my interest in the mind-body-spirit relationship and how it related to Sierra.

"Just tell the story," the writer said. "You don't need to combine it with anything. The story is powerful enough to stand on its own."

"Think of how your story can help people who have experienced loss," she continued. "You're an inspiration."

"Funny, I never thought of my story as something others could benefit from," I said. "I wanted to write it as a way of sorting through my own feelings."

As we said goodbye at the end of our last meeting, I finally knew what I had to do. I had to let Sierra's story out of its hiding place. I had to let the story take me by the hand and lead me toward the distant shore.

x.

In 2001 I finally began to write the story of Sierra. I found I couldn't delve into the story in my office at home. The pain of going back and reliving those early days meant I had to physically remove myself from my family and my normal life. I began taking writing retreats—sometimes to the Blue Ridge Mountains, other times to the Outer Banks—anywhere I could be alone with my thoughts, my pain.

A third visiting writer came to Old Dominion one fall to work with MFA students. This writer scared me a little. He'd written numerous books, penned articles for national magazines, and served as a judge for the National Book Awards. I gave him my memoir in progress to read, unsure what to expect, and waited for the designated day when we would discuss it.

We met at a café in Norfolk to go over my work. I arrived late that day, held up by traffic, worried about keeping him waiting. After settling into my chair, I waited for his comments.

"Powerful stuff," he said. He helped me see where my writing was honest and true and showed me places where the piece needed work. His comments made good sense. What puzzled me, though, was when he said that the story wasn't about Sierra.

"It's a love story," he said, "about you and Peter." I considered his remark. A love story? This sad tale about my daughter's death? How could this be a love story?

xi.

The day finally came. I submitted my manuscript to my thesis director and the other two professors on my thesis committee. I hoped I was done. But during my thesis defense, it became clear that I wasn't done. Although the professors believed the work had merit and granted my degree, what I had written was only the beginning.

I was tired of the story, though. I wanted it to be finished. The truth was I didn't want to relive that part of my life anymore. So I put the manuscript aside for a few months. That fall at a writer's conference I brought it out again and shared a few pages with an agent and a publisher. Both commented on the powerful writing and wanted to see the manuscript. Maybe this is it, I thought to myself. Maybe it is done and ready to be sent out into the world.

It wasn't. The publisher declined it with little comment. And the agent said, "Let's work on it some more." So I did. For a year

I buffed and polished, retooled and reshaped the piece. But in the end even the agent said it wasn't quite there yet.

Soon after, I attended a creative nonfiction conference and worked with extraordinary writers. Workshops, lectures, discussions coalesced, and all of a sudden, I knew what I needed to do. More scenes. More showing. Less telling.

I wrote a scene during the conference describing the day Peter and I scattered Sierra's ashes. I read it on the last night in front of a group of students and teachers. When I finished, the audience sat still and silent. I knew I was on the right track.

But it meant digging down deep again, going back into myself and looking once more at those moments when life grew dark.

The memoir still needed work.

So I set it aside again. For a year and a half I let it languish in a dusty box. Then I let the story out again.

Prologue

———*ᴐᴐᴐ*———

The long-ago scent of my daughter

Sierra's pink dress hangs in my closet. Now and then, as I slide the hangers back and forth, its pinkness peeks out at me, and I pause to caress the faded cotton fabric. Sometimes I lean over and press my nose against its soft folds, seeking the long-ago scent of my daughter.

Sierra's photograph brightens a wall in my office. She sits among the ruins of a church in West Virginia, wearing a teal t-shirt and a crooked smile. She's looking away from the camera, her large blue eyes focused elsewhere. "Why'd you look away?" I remember asking. "Let's try it again." But Sierra, who couldn't sit still for long, was already scrambling over a wall, seeking a new adventure.

Sierra's favorite book, a few plastic toys, some drawings, a pair of red shoes—these items sit in a box in my closet, precious things that connect me to her. Sometimes I open the box and examine the contents. As I touch each memento, I remember Sierra: the sound of her laughter, the way her fine blonde hair felt when I combed it, the smell of her breath.

I picture in my mind how she stood in the living room, hunched over the coffee table, clutching a crayon in her dimpled hand and making thick, deliberate strokes in her coloring book. Sometimes I can see her clearly, but as the years go by, her face becomes more blurred, her features less distinct. It gets harder and harder to conjure her up in my mind.

Sierra would be twenty-two now, but she died many summers ago in a swimming pool accident during a neighbor's party. She was almost three. My husband, Peter, and I were steps away from her when she drowned.

It was August 18, 1990, the day our world changed.

Now years later as I write the story about the impact of her death on my life, Sierra is all around me. Sitting in my house near the Virginia coast, I look across my backyard, where she climbed trees and splashed in mud puddles. Sierra is here, helping me write this story, guiding me, offering encouragement, especially when I get to the hard parts. It is after all her life and her death that consume me as I look back at the past and try to understand what happened and why.

Sierra lived for only two years, nine months, and eight days—a short interlude in the span of my life and my family's. Still Sierra's presence resonates within us every day. Even our sons—Scott, twenty-four; Jasper, twenty, and Ross, fifteen—acknowledge Sierra's place in our family: the sister whose photographs they know, whose voice they've heard on an old cassette tape, whose books they read. It's because her aura is still present in our home, a warm feeling that glows like the sun's last rays.

Sierra's the reason I'm telling this story, but this is not her story. It's my story and my family's. It's the story of our epic quest to figure out where we fit in, to discover what matters in the world, to explore the shape and meaning of happiness, that elusive state of being to which we all aspire.

Our journey begins and ends in the same place. In between, my family and I moved to another continent, traveled many thousands of miles, losing ourselves in new places, always searching for something.

This is the story of searching for happiness without Sierra.

Chapter 1

—◦◦◦—

Soft footsteps padding down the hall

The day Sierra died, I lost my temper with her. Twice. Even at two and a half, she was a willful child. Maybe being in the middle had something to do with it. Or maybe it was because she was the only girl. All I knew was, with three kids—Scott, who was four, Sierra, and Jasper, nine months—my patience wore thin some days, and this was one of those days.

Now resting my head on the back of the couch. I listened to the silence, closing my eyes for a moment. Good, I thought. Maybe she's finally asleep.

For the past hour, I'd been trying to put Sierra down for a nap without waking up Jasper, asleep in his crib.

Sierra was at that stage where she still needed naps but didn't want to take them. She'd rather play with her big brother, Scott, who was tinkering quietly with his Legos in another room.

Sierra didn't know how to play quietly. A busy child, she tended to be loud, boisterous, full of energy. I could use some of her energy right now. I felt completely drained.

That morning I had taken all three kids to a warehouse store. My husband, Peter, was running errands elsewhere. While Jasper rode in the shopping cart, Scott and Sierra toddled along, and I picked up milk and juice and bread. The store was crowded with Saturday shoppers, and I was in a hurry to get home so the kids could nap before we went to my neighbor's party that afternoon.

As we walked down the electronics aisle, Sierra stopped to watch a Beetlejuice cartoon. He was a ghostly character with blackened eyes and bad teeth who regularly survived all manner of bodily harm, always managing in the end to defy death with a cackling laugh.

My daughter stood and stared at the TV. "Come on, Sierra. We have to go," I said. Still she stood. I rolled the shopping cart back down the aisle, grabbed her hand firmly, and pulled her along. She whined, "I want to watch Beetlejuice." I picked her up, plunked her down in the cart, and headed for the checkout, trying not to lose my cool.

At home, Sierra was testing me again. I'd tried reading her stories, lying in bed with her, rubbing her back—everything I could think of to help her fall asleep. But she kept getting up. The last time she did, I swatted her bottom, carried her back to bed, and said crossly, "Now, go to sleep!" She started crying, of course, and I just knew Jasper would wake up from his nap.

But he didn't, and Sierra's crying eventually stopped. Now on the couch, I listened, barely breathing.

Then I heard it—soft footsteps padding down the hall.

Sierra.

With a tentative smile on her face, she climbed up onto my lap, looked at me with clear blue eyes, and said, "Mommy, can I please get up now?"

I didn't have the energy to fight with her anymore. "O.K. Sierra. Go play with your brother and try to be quiet, please." She jumped off my lap happily and ran down the hall, shouting for Scott. I sighed and waited for Jasper to stir.

The party was well underway when Peter, the kids, and I arrived. My neighbor, Kathy, had invited her brothers and their families, and there must have been ten kids running around. We were the only non-family people there. It was nice of Kathy and Rusty to include us. Scott and their son, Bucky, played together regularly, often taking a dip in their above-ground swimming pool, which sat between our two houses.

On this hot August afternoon, the pool was overflowing with laughing, splashing kids, while the adults watched, drinking beer and chatting. Peter and I stood poolside, too, taking turns holding Jasper, who squirmed in our arms, wanting to get down and crawl around. Sierra climbed out of the pool to grab a handful of potato chips, and she smiled at me. Though she wore a bulky lifejacket, I admired her muscular little body, thinking she'd make a fine athlete one day.

I noticed a car pulling up at our house next door and recognized a couple of our sales representatives getting out. Peter and I had just launched a new local magazine for parents, and we'd hired these two women to sell ad space for us.

"Do you want me to go over there and see what they want?" Peter asked.

"No, I'll go," I said, handing Jasper over. I wasn't happy about leaving the party. The women apologized for coming out on a Saturday and then explained that they'd decided not to work for us any longer. I wasn't surprised. Selling advertising is tough, especially for a new publication. But I was disappointed. We needed this business venture to succeed. It would be our main source of income since Peter had stopped his construction business due to a building slowdown.

The women apologized again. "It's OK," I said, anxious to return to the party.

When I got back next door, the pool was empty, kids scattered about. Peter was in the backyard with Jasper, who was crawling in the grass. "I think he's hungry," Peter said.

"I'll feed him inside where it's cool," I said and grabbed a bottle out of the diaper bag. Then Sierra appeared.

"Daddy, would you take off my life jacket?" she asked, "I want to play in the sand pile."

"Sure," he said and undid the buckles while I walked toward the house, carrying Jasper and the bottle of formula. I vaguely remember telling him to watch Sierra.

Moments later, I heard the scream. It sounded surreal, like one you'd hear in a scary movie. Loud and intense, it pierced the walls of Kathy's house, where I sat giving Jasper his bottle. I jumped up, handed my son to someone and rushed out into the humid afternoon. One of Kathy's brothers had jumped into the pool, and I saw a black bathing suit with colorful neon polka dots in the water.

Sierra.

Chapter 2

—◦◦◦—

Between life and death

When I saw Sierra's limp body being pulled from the pool, I dashed over to the phone, but I couldn't remember how to use it. Someone took the phone from me, and I ran back outside and stood on the wooden deck beside the pool under the hazy, late-afternoon sky. One of Kathy's brothers was performing CPR on Sierra. I tried to go to my daughter, but strong arms held me back.

Time stopped. People gathered. Someone took the other children into the house.

Out of nowhere Peter walked over to me and slammed his fist in my face. I fell backwards, stunned by the powerful punch. As I got up, I saw Kathy's brothers holding Peter as if he were an animal.

He began shouting at me, saying things like, "Why weren't you watching her?" I stood in a daze. Me watching her? I was inside giving Jasper a bottle. Why weren't you watching her?

My face burned. I'd never been hit like that before. My husband was a kind, loving man. Who was this monster shouting obscenities at me?

And there on the wooden deck lay the most beautiful girl in the world, poised between life and death. I had no idea which way she would go.

———⟳⟳⟳———

Life is full of choices. We make them every day. Simple decisions, like what to have for dinner, which road to take home, whether or not to buy that new pair of shoes. We also face bigger decisions, like whether to change careers or get married. We think about these longer, calculating our options.

Then there are those seemingly inconsequential decisions that punctuate our lives, the ones with lasting effects. Peter decided to take off Sierra's life jacket. I didn't say anything when I saw him do it. Peter decided to go play volleyball in the backyard. Sierra decided to go play in the sand pile. After a while she must have wanted to go swimming again to wash off the sand. She didn't realize she no longer had the life jacket on to keep her afloat.

I decided to go inside Kathy's house to give Jasper a bottle. It was cooler there. I could have chosen to sit by the pool and feed Jasper. I would have gotten sweaty, perhaps, but then my daughter wouldn't have drowned.

Seems a small price to pay for saving her life. A little sweat on a hot summer day.

———⟳⟳⟳———

The ambulance came from Sandbridge, a small beachfront community about five miles away. It took forever to arrive. I couldn't bear to stand around the pool and watch Sierra lying prone on the deck. I went into the front yard and waited for the ambulance. Collapsing in the grass, I beat on the hard ground with my bare fist and wailed, a sound like you hear Middle East women make on television when cameras film a death scene or a burial. I had no idea where my wailing came from—some primordial place deep inside.

The ambulance pulled up, and rescue workers rushed across the yard, carrying equipment. I followed them, recognizing a man from my church. They told everyone to stand back. I wanted to see. I wanted to be there when my daughter opened her eyes. But they made me go away. I stood on the porch with Kathy's mother and recited The Lord's Prayer. Over and over.

The rescue workers ran to the ambulance, carrying Sierra on a gurney. I caught a glimpse of her as they rushed by and saw they had ripped her bathing suit half off. No, I couldn't ride in the ambulance, they said. So Kathy grabbed her keys, and we jumped into her car. Kathy's mother said she would take care of Scott and Jasper.

Rusty took Peter in his car. My husband still hadn't spoken to me.

At a traffic light a mile down the road, Kathy stopped behind the ambulance, and we waited for what seemed an extraordinarily long time. The light changed from green to yellow to red over and over again while the ambulance remained motionless, its red lights splashing across our faces.

"Do you think they're working on her?" Kathy asked. I didn't answer.

Behind us tired, sunburned beachgoers, en route home after a day at the beach, began honking their horns. Anger rose up in my throat like bile. Didn't they know my daughter was in that ambulance and paramedics were fighting to keep her alive? How could they honk their horns?

Then the ambulance started moving again, a little more slowly it seemed. Kathy stopped for a red light at the next intersection, and the ambulance kept going.

At the hospital, someone led Kathy and me into a small nondescript room designed to provide privacy for people whose loved ones were somewhere in that nebulous place between life and death. Inside that room behind the closed door, we sat and waited. Someone called my mother, and she came into the little room, sat down, and began biting her nails. Kathy's minister arrived, too. He asked if I wanted to pray, but I shook my head.

Peter and Rusty sat outside on a picnic table. I watched my husband through a window. A gaping chasm separated us. He was a stranger now. I wasn't sure who he was anymore.

Finally a faceless doctor came into the room, sat down in a chair opposite me, and said, "She didn't make it. I'm sorry. We did everything we could." I sat, stunned, unable to process the information. I never thought Sierra would actually die.

A nurse said, "Do you want to see your daughter?"

"No," I said quietly. I did not want to see Sierra dead. What a thing to ask. My brain was still trying to send this message through the circuit board, but there was a breakdown somewhere. It was as if a loud buzzing alarm sounded in my brain in syncopated, bellowing bursts, drowning out everything else. An alarm that went off too late.

The nurse whispered to Kathy, who grabbed my arm and led me past swinging doors into the ER, saying, "You need to see her, Peggy. It's closure. You have to do it."

We stopped at a cubicle, pulled the curtain aside, and went in. I didn't touch her. I didn't kiss her. I could barely stand to look at her, lying in the hospital bed with transparent tubes in her nose, her eyes closed, her beautiful young body, pale and still.

Chapter 3

—⟨⟩⟨⟩⟨⟩—

A breath away

Peter shook his head and looked away when I told him he had to call his parents and tell them about the accident. It was the morning after Sierra drowned, and we'd sat up all night in the living room, avoiding each other's eyes.

My brother Tom had stayed with us, not talking, just being there. I wonder now if he was afraid Peter might lash out at me again. Sometime during the night I opened the Bible and read some psalms aloud, anything to make the time go by. Another time I tried to go rest in my bedroom, but I couldn't turn off the light. I couldn't stand the thought of being in the dark. So I sat on my bed alone and stared at the walls.

The sun came up the next morning amid a sky as pink as Sierra's favorite dress. I watched it from the front steps, drinking coffee and smoking—an old habit which was now a welcome friend. I stared at the front yard, where Sierra had played just yesterday. Now it was empty and still.

My brother called our dad and his wife, who immediately left their summer home in Canada and drove to Virginia, joining the many other family members and friends who surrounded us like a warm quilt those first terrible days.

I told Peter he had to call his parents and break the awful news to them.

"I can't," he said simply.

So I called the Netherlands. Peter's dad answered. After a moment's hesitation, I blurted out: "Sierra died. She drowned." It was the first time I'd said the words.

Piet said, "One moment," and put Peter's sister, Karin, on. Maybe he hadn't understood me, so I said it again to Karin, "Sierra died. She drowned." Then I gave the phone to Peter and left him to grieve with his family.

When Kathy brought Scott and Jasper home that morning, I grabbed them hungrily and held them in my arms like I was seeing them after a long absence. I had to tell Scott about his sister but had no idea what to say.

Luckily, I knew someone who could help: a hospice worker who'd called the week before to suggest an article about grieving children for *Tidewater Parent*, the monthly magazine Peter and I had just started. How ironic that someone who devoted her life to helping people deal with death contacted me only a few days before my family and I found ourselves facing our own unimaginable tragedy.

I called Jude and told her I needed help. She came over right away, wearing bright clothes and a brave smile.

Scott entered the living room, where Jude and I sat waiting. Then I told him Sierra died.

"Will she come back?" he asked, his voice quivering.

"No," I answered. "She won't ever come back."

Scott's face crumpled, and I held him a few moments. Suddenly, he brightened and began to toss a ball back and forth with Jude. He laughed and asked, "Can I go outside and play?" Then he was gone, and I wished I could be a child, too, and not have the terrible weight of reality to bear.

—⁓⁓—

When death occurs, a flurry of people follows in the wake. Neighbors bring casseroles; deliverymen bring flowers; people arrive from out of town who need to be welcomed and fed. It's easy to let events unroll, to feel like you're drifting in a current, out of control. Peter and I drifted like that in the beginning, like leaves in a swollen creek. The only time it got quiet was at night. My husband and I would lie silently in our king-sized bed, facing away from each other. If we spoke at all, it was only what needed to be said and nothing more.

Peter's mom and sister flew over from the Netherlands. Photos we took during their visit show us posing with frozen smiles. In one we're all lined up in the kitchen, pretending this is just another family gathering. In another I sit on a picnic table under a crabapple tree in our front yard, smoking, surrounded by college friends who came to comfort, a smile on my face, a black semicircle under my left eye.

That day we'd held Sierra's memorial service at Sandbridge Community Chapel. The minister, Ed Martin, and my friend Linda helped put together a simple ceremony. Linda read one of Sierra's favorite books about a little girl who sails off to faraway places at night while she sleeps. As Ed played the guitar, we sang, "Jesus Loves Me" and "Michael, Row The Boat Ashore," but there was no comfort in the words.

One evening that first week I stopped at a grocery store to buy milk. The cheerful girl at the cash register asked, "How're you doing?" as she rang up my purchase. I had to bite my lip. You really want to know how I'm doing? I wanted to answer. Well, my daughter drowned a few days ago, my husband gave me this black eye, I feel like my life is over, and by the way, how're you doing?

Of course, I couldn't blame this poor girl for my troubles, but her innocent question made me think. How are we doing? What's really behind the smiles on our faces? As I floundered through my own grief, I learned almost everyone has a sad story to tell. A painful divorce, an alcoholic parent, a sister with cancer, a stillborn child. Tragedy is a breath away from all of us.

—◦◦◦—

Peter said we should cremate Sierra's body. He had left the planning of the memorial service up to me, but he had strong feelings about cremation.

"But if we bury Sierra—I mean, her body—in a grave somewhere, I can go and visit and remember her," I said. "It will be a place to connect with her."

This was the first time we had discussed anything important since the accident.

"Peggy, it's better if you don't have a place that you have to go visit," Peter said. "What if we move one day? You'll always feel like you need to come back here and visit her grave."

I understood what he was saying, but the thought of cremation—the fire, the burning, the ashes—and Sierra's beautiful body—her hair, her lips, her fingers and toes. I couldn't bear to think of it.

A couple days later Peter and I walked down a sandy trail in Back Bay Wildlife Refuge south of Sandbridge, dressed in t-shirts and shorts. Sweat glistened on our faces, and buzzing deerflies darted about.

Ed, our minister, walked between us, wearing black pants and a black short-sleeved shirt, his cleric collar exposing a small white rectangle at his throat. In his hands he carried a black plastic box about four inches square.

We walked south under the glaring sun. Fields of brown and gold grass swept out in every direction. To the east pale white dunes blocked the ocean breeze. In the west, marshes gave way to the shallow gray waters of Back Bay.

Occasionally hikers and bicyclists passed by. Ed smiled and nodded at them, but Peter and I stared straight ahead.

We came here to spread her ashes because Sierra loved the wildlife refuge. I'd brought the children here often for hikes, Jasper in a backpack, Scott and Sierra walking beside me. But Sierra didn't walk, really. She trotted, she bounded, she raced, she skipped.

Once she disappeared during a hike. I panicked and ran to find her. As I rounded a bend in the trail, there she stood, calmly waiting for me, smiling her gap-toothed grin. I started to scold and then bent down and folded my arms around her, burying my face in her fine blonde hair.

———✺———

The perfect spot appeared.

"Over there," I said and pointed to a small grove of trees— pines, live oaks, shrubs, an oasis of green.

Ed, Peter, and I entered the cool darkness and stood under the canopy in front of a sandy spot. Ed prayed, "Heavenly Father, we are gathered here today in memory of Sierra." When the prayer ended, Peter and I shook the ashes out of the box and watched the chalky flecks drift slowly to the ground.

Peter knelt, his shoulders hunched over, and wept quietly. I could only stare, dry eyed, at the random pattern of ashes that used to be my daughter.

Chapter 4

—⁓—

Finding our way

Books about bereavement say that while everyone grieves differently, a rough pattern usually emerges. It starts with numbness and disbelief, followed by anger, then guilt and depression, and eventually, for those who work toward it, recovery.

Numbness was best. Missy, a college friend, came by soon after Sierra died. I met her on the sidewalk in front of my house, and we hugged. Missy shook with emotion in my arms. Dry-eyed, I comforted her. This scene played out over and over in those early days.

I took a walk with Cindy, another college friend, sometime that first week. We sat on a log in the woods, and Cindy wept while I watched. I tried to cry, but I couldn't. I remember Cindy saying, "Peggy, of all the people this had to happen to, you're so strong. I know you'll be fine." I was amazed: everyone else seemed sadder than I was.

Of course, the sadness would come, but before it did, anger surfaced. I was furious with God. Until Sierra died, I prayed each night, asking God to keep my children safe. I blamed God for Sierra's death. Why hadn't he been watching her?

Blaming God was the easiest thing to do. He didn't live in my house, sleep in my bed, or sit across from me at breakfast. It would be a while before I would be able to think about blaming anyone else. God was the perfect scapegoat.

I still attended church because I needed a sense of connection to Sierra. I believed that I would see her again one day in heaven. But in the meantime I was very angry at God. And when the congregation sang, "Praise God From Whom All Blessings Flow," I remained silent.

I didn't know it then, but other angry feelings were simmering in the soup, slowly bubbling to the surface.

—◦◦◦—

When I was twenty-four, my mother and I traveled through Europe together. We hopscotched across the continent, spending a few days each in Germany, Austria, Italy, France, and Belgium, before landing in the Netherlands, where we stayed three nights in a hotel in Amsterdam near Dam Square.

There a friendly waiter named Peter with blue eyes and an easy laugh served breakfast in the morning and fixed a tasty Irish coffee in the bar at night.

I loved Amsterdam's vibrant atmosphere, its colorful flowers and noisy, crowded streets, and wanted to stay longer, but Mom and I were scheduled to visit my brother, Dick, in Sweden. I said goodbye to Peter and wondered if I'd ever see him again.

I didn't wonder long. A week later, after leaving Mom behind in Sweden, I headed south to visit friends in Belgium, stopping in Amsterdam en route. I booked a room in the same hotel, and there was Peter, waiting, as though he'd known I was coming back.

That night he invited me out for a drink. On a floating patio under the moonlight, we sat across from each other, shy, not talking much at first, then casually conversing, and suddenly exploding with ideas and sharing our dreams and letting our hearts speak about what life meant to us and what we hoped to be and do. The moon drifted across the black sky, our chairs swayed as a gentle breeze blew, and I became intoxicated by the music of Peter's voice and the place where we were and the dizzy feeling that my life might now no longer be my own.

We said farewell amid trembling kisses on the sidewalk in front of the hotel as the sky turned purple and pink, and then I returned to Sweden. I remember sitting on my brother's porch on a chilly evening as the sun settled over the shadowy hillside, trying to decide whether to send Peter a casual, friendly letter or to write what my heart felt. I wrote a love letter, and two weeks later back in Virginia, to my delight, I received one from him.

That was the beginning of a two-year courtship across the Atlantic. In my small house in the farmlands of Virginia Beach, I wrote to my faraway Dutchman. Our letters were tentative at first, but grew more passionate as the months passed by. The following summer I took another trip to Europe, a two-month backpacking adventure, this time with a friend named Mugsy. I scheduled a week to visit Peter.

No longer in Amsterdam, he lived in a small town called Vriescheloo in the northeast corner of the Netherlands. He and his sister had bought a café, and they lived with their parents in an adjoining house. I was nervous about meeting Peter's family, but they seemed happy to welcome Mugsy and me for a visit. After a couple days, Mugsy left to pursue solo traveling, but I stayed put, and love took hold.

A year later in 1984, I moved to the Netherlands to live with Peter. It was a heady time, leaving my job, my family and friends, my single life behind and skipping across the ocean to settle in a different world with a man I hardly knew.

But I loved Peter. I loved his quick smile, his certainty, his ambition, his sensitivity. I loved how close he was to his family. I loved how he brought me flowers and took me to dinner. I loved how he dressed in a suit and tie with a silk scarf around his neck. I loved how he wooed me and caressed my skin and kissed me on the cheek and neck and in secret places.

I gladly left my ordinary American life for a dashing Dutchman who had drive, charm, and good looks. I knew our life would be an adventure.

—◦◦◦—

After the memorial service, friends and family disappeared. I hated to see them go. Peter and I had to put out the September issue of *Tidewater Parent*. August 1990 had been our premiere issue, in which I had introduced myself as the new editor and an experienced mother of three children.

Now I faced a decision. Should I tell my readers about Sierra's death in my "Parent to Parent" column? The answer was how could I not? Soon after the September issue hit the streets, the phone began to ring. People were shocked and called to say how sorry they were and how brave I was to tell my story. The daily newspaper called and wanted to write an article about Peter and me, the irony of our situation a perfect subject for a human interest story. The article, titled "Working It Out," appeared less than a month after Sierra died and resulted in more phone calls and letters. Peter and I became known for our loss, which had somehow become everyone's loss.

The business gave us a focus, but Peter and I continued to behave like strangers, each of us in a deep well, wondering whether we could climb out.

We still didn't talk. We barely touched each other. Numb to all of our feelings, we kept our distance. Three out of four couples who experience the death of a child divorce, we learned. I didn't want to join those bereaved couples whose marriages fell apart, but I began to feel a growing sense of anger toward Peter. We needed to talk about the day of the accident.

Somehow I wanted Peter to take responsibility for Sierra's death; then I wouldn't feel so guilty. After all, he took off her life jacket and stayed outside to play volleyball in the yard beside the pool. He should have been watching her.

Lauren, a close friend, met me for lunch on a warm fall day a couple months after Sierra died, and I told her how I felt. Sitting on an outdoor terrace at a restaurant in Norfolk, I wondered what people would think if they listened to our conversation. They chatted happily at tables around us, oblivious to the dark secrets I shared with my friend.

"Do you think he'll admit he's responsible?" Lauren asked.

I didn't know. Peter tended to be self-assured—some might say arrogant—and rarely admitted to wrongdoing. I could probably count on one hand the times he'd said he was sorry to me during the five years we'd been married. But I didn't mind this small character flaw. Peter's good sides were many: he was generous and kind, a loving father, my best friend. In general, we had a good marriage, and until Sierra died, our lives held great promise.

"How do I even bring up the subject?" I asked Lauren.

She shrugged and said, "But this will eat you up inside, Peggy. You have got to say something."

So I did. One night in bed. In the dark. I don't remember the exact words I said or what he said. I remember we both cried. Finally in a husky voice, Peter whispered, "O.K., it's my fault," and then he turned away from me, struggling to control his emotions.

Hearing him say he was responsible did not make me feel better. I would still carry guilt in the crook of my arm for months and years to follow. But during our brief talk, we moved a step closer to finding our way back to each other again.

Soon afterwards we made love for the first time since the accident. In our bed, where for months we'd lain with our backs barely touching, tormented, not sure how to face each other again, we came together, both of us crying and holding each other and letting the waves of emotion roll over us. Opening our bodies up to pleasure also opened the raw wounds that festered inside us, and as our bodies became entangled, so too did our feelings—anger, heartache, love, sadness, shame, guilt, hope, joy.

When it was over, we lay, spent and empty.

We crossed an invisible boundary that night, a demarcation between the past and the future. But we still had a long way to go.

Chapter 5

—◦◦◦—

Beyond tears

The idea of moving away was always there—even from the beginning. In a different place, where Sierra had never been, we would be able to start over. Living in the same house where she had slept, eaten, cried, played, and brightened my days was too hard. Nothing felt right. Everything felt wrong. And there in my neighbor's yard stood the pool where my daughter drowned. I saw it every day.

I shared my feelings with a woman I met at Compassionate Friends, a support group for bereaved parents. Just a few weeks after Sierra died, Peter and I began attending monthly meetings. These became an outlet for us, a place where we felt safe, where others understood how mixed up we were. To my surprise, Peter broke down at almost every meeting, sobbing, unable to hold back the tears, not caring if anyone saw him. He needed this release. And though I rarely cried there, I found solace in sharing memories of Sierra.

This mother's young son had drowned in a river behind her home, and I asked, "Don't you want to move? Isn't it hard to live in that house so near where your son died?"

She answered with a firm shake of her head, saying that she'd much rather stay there because that's where his presence was. If she moved away, she'd lose her connection with him.

I nodded in understanding. Of course, I didn't want to forget Sierra or the time we had together. And, yes, selling our house would mean saying goodbye to Sierra in a sense because her laughter echoed within those walls, and outside in the yard her shadow peeked from behind the pines. I did feel closer to her there, and I'd miss that feeling if we left.

So we stayed put and sought other ways to fill the void in our lives. One way was to have another baby, preferably a girl. Bringing a new life into the world seemed like a healing thing—not to replace the one that was taken, but to try to recapture some of the elusive joy we once knew. Getting pregnant turned out to be harder now than it used to be. When we finally conceived, keeping the baby proved difficult, too. I miscarried in 1992 and again in 1993. Each time I was saddened, but not devastated, perhaps since losing these tiny beings did not begin to approach the pain of losing Sierra.

Because once the numbness wore off, sadness swooped down like a vulture that picked away at my insides. I learned what raw pain is like. It's waking up in the morning and thinking for a moment that you've just had a terrible dream. Then you realize your worst nightmare has come true. And a weight crashes down, a huge boulder, and falls on your heart, smashing it. Tears don't even figure in. This sorrow is beyond tears.

You lose yourself in the intensity of it for a few seconds, maybe a minute, and then you draw upon some small ounce of strength to rise up out of your bed, start coffee, wake children, and begin another day. You wear a mask because the ugliness of your pain is way too scary to show anyone. It stays hidden, and you deal with it.

A series of au pairs helped us get through those first few years. I worked part time for a foreign exchange organization and planned to get an au pair to help care for my children before Sierra died.

In fact, the morning of August 18, 1990, I confirmed my match with a German girl named Katharina. I remember telling Sierra about her new "big sister" that morning. Sierra always asked a lot of questions and seemed unusually wise for such a little girl.

"What's her name?" Sierra asked, her large blue eyes looking up at me.

"Kat-ha-ri-na," I answered. "She's from Germany, the country next to Holland where Oma and Opa and Tante Karin live." Peter's parents and sister had visited us the previous summer, and we talked often about our faraway relatives.

"Where will she sleep?"

"She'll have her own room right beside yours and Scotty's," I answered. We were getting in the car to run some errands before lunch, so we could be back in time for naps before Kathy and Rusty's party that afternoon.

"Will she play with me?" Sierra asked. "Will she take me to the park?"

"Yes, and she'll help take care of your brothers, too."

"Will she talk English?"

I nodded.

"How long will she be here?

"She's only allowed to stay a year and then another girl will come live with us," I told her.

But Katharina didn't last her full year with us. In fact, she didn't last a month. My friend Lauren, who also worked for the exchange organization, called Katharina in Germany a few days after Sierra died and told her she could back out if she wanted to. For some reason Katharina came anyway, but after two weeks, she asked to be assigned to another family. To no one's surprise, she couldn't cope with the sadness in our house.

After Katharina left, Joanna joined our family. She was a stoic Brit, almost six feet tall, who'd known some sadness in her life and was prepared to cope with ours. And she did a brave job, but ended up coming down with mono after seven months, so we were left alone again.

Next came Rena, a native Inuit from Greenland with black hair, freckles, and a wide toothy smile. She was the youngest in a family of eight and proved to be the hardest worker among the au pairs we hosted. More than just efficient, Rena was incredibly loving at a time when Peter and I needed affection. She always kissed us when she went out, and we grew to love her as though she were our own daughter. In a way Rena helped fill the void Sierra left. Having another female in the house, especially one so affectionate, was a tonic. She knew we hurt deeply and did everything she could to bring joy into the house.

"Why don't you and Peter go out tonight?" she'd suggest. Or she encouraged us to take off for the weekend, recognizing that Peter and I needed time alone to recapture the closeness we had known before Sierra died. We never took that weekend getaway, reluctant perhaps to leave Scott and Jasper behind. Or maybe we weren't ready to spend so much time together, worried that the pain—still so raw and close to the surface—would be more than we could bear in a quiet place, away from the hectic pace of family life. Perhaps the au pairs we hosted served as a safety zone for us, a buffer that gave Peter and me the time and space we needed to learn to trust each other again.

During Rena's year with us, we marked the one-year anniversary of Sierra's death. Family and friends joined Peter and me and our sons at my mother's beach house. On the screened porch we told stories and read poetry and cried and laughed. We shared food and beer and wine. It was a celebration of sorts, a pat on the back for Peter and me. We'd made it through the hardest year of our lives and could only hope that things would improve.

The months and years that trickled by brought little relief, however. Sometimes it seemed we were actors starring in an endless movie, a bad movie without a plot or any character development. We went through the motions of life and waited and hoped for a happy ending.

In the mid-90s, our involvement with au pairs ended. While most of the girls had enriched our lives, providing much-needed help and friendship, two in a row had proven unacceptable—one a German girl who dressed in black and never smiled, the other a Dutch girl who was fond of beer—and we decided we didn't need au pairs anymore.

I became pregnant again toward the end of 1994, and this one took. While I hadn't wanted to know the sex of any of my previous children beforehand, I needed to know this one's. Peter made the call, and as soon as I heard his voice change, I knew the baby wasn't a girl. I ran into the bathroom, locked the door, and wept because I knew this would be the last child for us, and I'd never have a daughter again.

Chapter 6

—◦◦◦—

Feelings of restlessness

Like a gathering storm, feelings of restlessness brewed with each passing year. We left Virginia Beach for frequent trips with our sons, traveling to Europe in 1993, to Florida, the Midwest, Canada, Vermont, Pennsylvania, the Gulf Coast, and New York City. In 1995, when I was eight and a half months pregnant and lumbering around like an elephant, we attended a family reunion in Cincinnati. Lucky for us, the baby didn't come early.

When Ross did come that August, almost five years to the day that Sierra died, the tempo of life quickened as we added caring for a newborn to our already busy lives. I loved being a mother again, nursing Ross and watching him learn to smile and crawl and walk and talk. That year we also built an addition to our home; three offices and a half bath lengthened the front of our one-story ranch, offering more space to accommodate the staff we hired to help us run our growing business. Working at home had its downside, however, since job responsibilities called us from the next room, and Peter and I regularly put in long hours.

That's why our trips became so important. Escaping to new places began to take on more meaning than our everyday existence. Of course, most people relish time off from work. Vacations refresh the spirit and often lead to a better perspective upon returning, perhaps even a renewed appreciation for being home again, immersed in the normal routine of life. But for Peter and me, returning from our trips didn't offer that satisfaction. We'd come back home only to find that same empty feeling and begin planning the next trip almost immediately.

It's not that our business was unrewarding. *Tidewater Parent* had succeeded in becoming an important regional resource for area parents. In my monthly column "Parent to Parent," I offered my own perspectives on family life.

From the beginning I had written regularly about Sierra and how my family was coping with her death. Expressing my feelings through my columns was one way of coping with my sadness. I also believed I had to be honest with my readers. How could I not write about Sierra when every time my eyes blinked, I felt the impact of her death and her brief life on my own?

Our lives, it seemed, were always being brought back to Sierra. Sometimes it was our own doing that brought us face to face with her again, such as the times I wrote about her life or the tragedy of her death in my columns. Other times out of nowhere something would cause the sadness and grief that had lain dormant to return with a biting sharpness.

Once I wrote in "Parent to Parent" about my 20-year high school reunion and how disturbed I had been about the silly awards given for the most marriages and most jobs held. I mentioned how success in anything—relationships, the workplace, life in general—is a result of hard work and that too often people lack the tenacity to succeed. Instead, they give up. Then I wrote that the grief work I had done in the years following Sierra's death was some of the hardest work I'd ever done, but that I was stronger for having done it.

Soon after that issue came out, I was standing in line at a fast-food restaurant in Norfolk when a woman next to me smiled and introduced herself, saying, "Hi, you're the editor of *Tidewater Par-*

ent, aren't you? I just read your column about your high school reunion. I'm having my 20-year reunion this year, so I really related to what you wrote."

A day or two later I received a note in the mail from the same woman. "I hadn't read the entire column when I saw you," she wrote, "and that night after I read about your daughter's death, I felt terrible for not saying something. Please accept my deepest sympathy." These kinds of connections occurred frequently between me and my readers, resurrecting the ache.

Then there were the dreams. Each night I went to bed hoping I would see Sierra in my dreams. When I did, I never wanted to wake up. On those lucky nights, Sierra was her old self again—and so was I. Dressed in her blue-jean coveralls, cheeks pink and glowing, her wide grin stretching across her face, she'd climb into my lap for a hug. I'd wrap my arms around her warm body, squeeze her tight, and smile, feeling whole again. Then the dream would end, and I'd wake up with empty arms. Sometimes I would even acknowledge in my dreams that I was dreaming and try to stay there as long as I could—but ultimately I'd awaken once more to be the woman whose daughter drowned in a pool when she wasn't looking.

Sierra's death continued to define my life.

To some it may have seemed that the time for grieving had passed. Years had slipped by, yet the memory of Sierra's death still saturated our lives: images Peter and I could never forget because we lived next door to where it all happened. And every year on August 18, we relived that gut-wrenching summer afternoon.

But there were happy memories, too: Sierra climbing the crabapple tree in our yard and hiding among the pink blossoms or playing house with Scott, her dolls perched in Jasper's high chair as she fed them imaginary food and cooed baby talk. Or dancing on our lawn in the shadowy evening sunlight a week before she died. Wearing a pink dress, her blonde hair tumbling about her ears, she twirled faster and faster before falling in a heap beside her big brother, both of them breathless with laughter as Jasper crawled in the grass nearby.

From our lawn chairs, Peter and I laughed at their antics, enjoying the simple pleasures of a summer day, unaware a change was coming that would leave us breathless, too, and sobbing in our pillows, trying not to let each other hear.

The good memories hurt worse than the bad ones.

That's why we kept leaving—taking trips somewhere, anywhere, just to get away, to focus our thoughts on something, anything, other than the haunting memories of our little girl. School and work always called us back, however, back to the place that used to be home. Maybe if we stayed away longer, we thought, maybe if we went further.

A four-week trip to Europe seemed like a good idea, albeit an adventurous one with three young boys. So in 1996 Peter and I took Scott, ten; Jasper, six; and Ross, barely one, on a summer vacation that looped from France to Sweden and back again, with stops along the way in Belgium, Holland, Germany, and Denmark.

Trying to lose ourselves in the sights and sounds of Paris, we climbed the Eiffel Tower, explored Notre Dame, and watched the sidewalk artists of Montmartre. An old accordion player, cigarette dangling from his smiling lips, serenaded us with a familiar French tune. Street performers juggled while we dined on an outdoor terrace. Boats wafted down the Seine amid sparkling diamonds, reflections of the summer sun.

I thought about how much Sierra would have loved the tempo of Paris and wondered what she would have been like as a teenager, a young woman. Anytime I saw a mother and daughter together, I ached inside. My time with Sierra wasn't long enough. I felt cheated. Whenever I spotted girls that reminded me of her, I'd think, That's about how old Sierra would be. Or I'd wonder what she'd look like now. Would her hair still be blonde? Would she have grown tall? Would she still have her easy smile, her sunny laughter, her stubborn streak?

That summer in Paris, we started a family ritual. The five of us walked into the cool darkness of the Sacré Coeur Basilica and lit a candle for Sierra. Silently we thought about her, felt close to her in that solemn old marble monument. As we traveled that summer through Europe, Scott and Jasper would often remind Peter and me to stop and pay homage when we walked by a church. Our young sons sensed somehow the soothing effect this ritual had on all of us. Lighting candles and sending silent greetings to Sierra kept us in touch with her while we traveled and provided an opportunity to welcome Sierra back into our midst without dredging up the pain and sorrow we endured every day at home.

Later as Scott and Jasper romped in a playground near the Sacré Coeur and Ross slept peacefully in the stroller, I said to Peter, "I could live here." We sat on a wooden bench, listening to a tinkly carousel tune and the happy shouts of children. As the sun warmed our skin, we relaxed, feeling a sense of freedom.

"Look at Scott and Jasper playing with those French kids," I said. "They could adjust to moving here. They're young. They can learn a new language."

"You want to move to France?" Peter asked.

"Maybe," I answered, "or Holland. I don't know. I just want to try living in Europe and let the kids learn more about the world."

"Peg, this is a big decision," Peter said. "Think about all the logistics of moving overseas. Plus we'd have to sell our business."

Tidewater Parent had by then grown to become a valuable entity. As members of a national trade organization called Parenting Publications of America, we knew buyers were easy to find for magazines like ours.

"We could start over, Peter. We could get jobs or start a new business. I could teach in an international school. We can do it. The kids are young. It's the perfect time!"

"Starting over isn't that easy, Peg," Peter said, his blue eyes gazing intently into mine. "And besides we might not like living in Europe. It might not work. And remember we're on vacation now. Sightseeing and picnicking and café sitting aren't the same as working and paying bills and keeping house."

"Yes, but think about how in Holland everyone has four weeks' paid vacation. And shorter work weeks. The change would do us all good," I said. "It's just what we need."

I wanted to say, It's just what we need now that Sierra's gone. It's just what we need to be happy again. I didn't say it, though. While Sierra was always in our hearts and on our minds and even though we did mention her by name almost every day, remembering something she did or including her in the boys' bedtime prayers, Peter and I didn't often speak about the vacant place inside of us, the sadness we tried to escape when we took off on vacations like this one, or the emptiness waiting for us when we got home.

Home wasn't home anymore, and I didn't think it ever would be. Sierra's death was too near, literally and figuratively. I wanted to start fresh in a place where I could shed the sad aura that seemed to envelop us in Virginia. I'd finally come to realize that I wasn't connecting with the people in my life. Sadness had become a shield, separating me from my children and my husband. It was as if I saw them from a vast distance, observing but not interacting. I stayed apart from them because I didn't want to be hurt again.

The trips we took offered us the chance to forget our sadness, to lose ourselves in the excitement of new places. Sometimes, as on our trip to Europe in 1996, the luster would come back, dazzling and brilliant, blinding us in its intensity, and our hearts would grow glad again.

Hiding behind my shield was keeping me weak. Soon a growing sense of restlessness would compel me to leave the comforting shadowlands and emerge, squinting in the strong sunlight.

Chapter 7

─◦◦◦─

Sharing hopes and dreams

After we left Paris, we traveled to the Netherlands, where we joined Peter's parents at a bungalow park near the German border. I loved the spacious wooden house we rented with its red roof tiles, sleek modern furniture, and feather comforters. Despite the cool, rainy weather that clouded our week there, we relished our time with Oma, Opa, and Tante Karin, swimming in the indoor pool, taking long walks, and exploring nearby towns.

Though tempted, we chose not to tell Peter's family we were thinking of moving to Europe. We'd disappointed them once before in 1987 when Scott was a toddler and I was pregnant with Sierra. Peter and I considered our busy lives in the States and decided living on one income in the Netherlands was feasible and would allow me to be a stay-at-home mom. Peter's family was overjoyed. However, before we could solidify our plans, Peter received a promotion at work, which enticed us to stay in the U.S. We didn't want to disappoint them again.

Scott and Jasper played easily with Dutch children at the bungalow park, and I found myself thinking, "See, they could adapt to living here."

I even brought up the subject to Scott and Jasper one evening after dinner, a gentle inquiry, just to see how they would react.

"What would you think about living in Holland?" I asked Scott as we washed dishes in the bungalow while Peter gave Ross a bath. "I don't think I'd like it," Scott said.

"Me, either," Jasper called from the couch, where he was watching Dutch cartoons.

"Why not?" I asked.

"We can't speak Dutch," Scott answered.

"Well, if you went to an international school, you wouldn't have to. They speak English there."

"What's an international school?" Jasper asked.

"Well, it's where the kids of business people from different countries go to school when they live in Holland. You'd meet kids from all over the world," I said.

"What about soccer?" Scott asked.

"You could keep playing. Soccer's a big sport in Holland, but here they call it 'voetball.'"

"What about my friends?" Jasper asked.

"You could write them letters, and they could come visit," I said.

"I don't think I want to move to Holland," Scott said.

"Me, either," Jasper echoed.

"I like Virginia Beach," Scott said.

"Me, too," Jasper said.

"Well, sometimes, it's good to try new things," I said and thought to myself, They can be persuaded.

———❧———

From the Netherlands, we drove through German forests and pastoral countryside north to the Baltic Sea, where we caught a ferry to southern Sweden to visit my brother and his family at their quaint farmhouse near the coast.

Ever since traveling to Dick's the summer I met Peter, I envied his European lifestyle. He married Nilla, a Swedish woman he met when she was an exchange student in the U.S. Theirs had been a long-distance relationship for many years until finally the pull became too strong, and Dick moved to Sweden to be with Nilla in the late 70s. After their first son, they had a daughter and another son, and while they complained of high taxes, they seemed content to live in their little Swedish home nestled in the hilly farmland near the Baltic. Or so we thought.

"We're thinking about coming to America for a year," Dick said after dinner as we sat in their front yard, watching the yellow wheat fields ripple in the evening breeze.

"What? Where?" I asked, surprised. I thought Dick and his family loved their simple lifestyle in Sweden. Dick worked as a caretaker of two old-as-the-Vikings churches in nearby villages. He helped with Sunday services, burials, and weddings and maintained the buildings and the grounds. Dick's job gave him a lot of time to be with the children since Nilla worked full time as a physical therapist. He also had a small woodworking business on the side.

"We're not sure," Dick said slowly, rubbing his gray-flecked beard. "We just want to try it for a year. Nilla might want to get her physical therapist's license in Virginia. That way if we ever wanted to move to the U.S., she could get a good job." Dick and Nilla, it seemed, felt caught between two continents just as Peter and I did.

Of my four brothers, Dick was the one I identified with most. He listened to his heart. When he was drafted during the Vietnam War in the early 70s, he followed his conscience instead and traveled around the world, a fugitive on the run. I remember receiving letters from far-off places: Egypt, India, Australia, South America. During a round-the-world sailing race, he sent home a wooden cross he'd carved for me during the long, lonely hours crossing the ocean under sail. But Dick loved America, and when the option presented itself, he returned and served two years of community service, glad to be able to work off his debt to his country.

When Sierra died, Dick called from Sweden and asked if I wanted him to come. Knowing that money was tight, I said no, but he came anyway, sensing I needed him.

One evening during his visit, Dick knocked at my bedroom door. I was hiding from the world, probably reading one of the many books by bereaved parents I found in the public library. I devoured those books in the first few weeks, hoping for a clue about how everything would turn out.

Dick came in and started talking about stories he'd read. His love of literature matched mine, and soon we were talking about James Joyce and his short stories, one in particular called "The Dead," an odd tale that deals with love and dreams and forgiveness and how we always seem to be striving for something. While talking about the story, I forgot to be sad for a few minutes, letting Dick's presence, his calm soothing voice, wash over me.

As the sun slowly settled in the hills behind Dick and Nilla's cozy house in Sweden, I told them about our dream to move to Europe. We discussed the possibility of trading houses, but it didn't seem practical, especially since Peter and I felt that if we ever left Virginia Beach, we would never return. A cloud hung low over that place, and we believed leaving our old home behind was the only way we could feel at home anywhere.

———⟨⟩———

Following our visit to Sweden, Peter, our sons, and I continued on to Bremen, Germany, to visit an exchange student named Grit, whom I'd befriended in the late 80s. Her parents were away on holiday, so Grit invited us to stay in their picturesque home in a flower-filled suburb.

One morning as Grit and I walked together to a nearby farm for fresh milk, I confided in her about my dream to move to Europe.

"Won't you just be trying to run away from your unhappiness?" Grit asked. She knew Sierra, having babysat her and Scott occasionally when she was in the U.S.

"Well, what if we are?" I countered. "Is that so bad?"

Grit answered in her measured English, only a slight accent betraying her heritage, "I think your sadness may follow you wherever you go."

Grit's direct manner startled me, but I had to admit she was probably right. Moving to a new place might not be the way to get rid of my sadness and uncertainty, but I wanted to try. At the very least, it would be an adventure. And if things worked out the way I hoped, a new kind of happiness might enter our lives, replacing the emptiness Sierra had left behind.

There was something else at work, too, a sentiment I didn't immediately acknowledge, but it swam beneath the surface as Peter and I discussed in greater depth the possibility of moving to Europe. What finally motivated us to leave—more than running away from the past—was the lesson Sierra's death taught Peter and me. We learned the hard way how tenuous life is and how swiftly and suddenly sadness can swoop down and clutch you in its claws.

As time passed, I began to think more frequently about seeking pleasure in life as a goal in and of itself. After experiencing the deep, jolting sadness of Sierra's death, I believed I deserved happiness more than the average person. This seize-the-day mentality began to dominate my thought processes. Everything else became secondary.

—◁◉◉◉▷—

After our return from Europe, I found myself daydreaming more and more about moving to the Netherlands with its cozy homes, tulips, and trains. I pictured my boys riding bikes through the countryside, attending international school, playing soccer with Dutch kids, becoming more worldly.

I wrote the headmasters of a few international schools in the

Netherlands about possible teaching positions, figuring if I could find a job, Peter would be more inclined to make this move. The schools wrote back saying there were no vacancies at present, but the international school in Maastricht sent me a surprisingly warm letter, saying there were no openings currently, but they would keep my resumé on file. The school there, as well as the international community, looked inviting.

Peter and I had explored Maastricht during a visit to Europe the summer of 1993—before Ross was born. We left Scott and Jasper in the care of Peter's folks and boarded a southbound train. As we rolled through the flat countryside, I realized this was the first time Peter and I had been alone—just the two of us—since before Sierra died. It felt right, as if we were finally able to enjoy being a couple again.

I loved the southern side of the Netherlands—so charming and utterly different from the rest of the country. Here the landscape wasn't defined by fields and fences, cows and canals, windmills and wide, flat spaces stretching from sunrise to sunset. In the south, apple orchards, horse pastures, river bluffs, and green hills undulated in every direction, creating landscapes worthy of Van Gogh's brushstrokes.

During our brief interlude away from the kids, Peter and I found our way back to each other again. Strolling along cobblestone streets, holding hands; sitting in sunny outdoor cafés beside the Maas River, sipping wine; and driving through the rolling countryside, pointing out pretty houses, we shared our hopes and dreams once more and talked about our past—and our future.

Chapter 8

—∞∞∞—

A giant wave

"How about living in Maastricht?" I asked Peter one evening in the fall of 1996. We sat in a local restaurant, enjoying a rare night out. Ever since we stopped having au pairs, we had to compete for babysitters like everyone else.

"Maastricht sounds good," Peter answered, "but I'd still rather move to the South of France."

"I hear you," I said, "but you know Holland. You know the culture and the laws—not to mention the language. It'll be easier to start a business there. You've done it before. Plus we'll be near your family, and you always say you wish they could see more of the kids."

This conversation continued in myriad forms that fall over the kitchen table, in the car, in the bedroom, and in the office until one day Peter surprised me by saying, "All right, Peggy, you win. We'll move to Holland, but you have to be sure this is what you want to do. You can't change your mind once I put everything in motion." He meant, of course, selling *Tidewater Parent*, an essential step in our moving plans since our business represented most of our assets, not counting a little equity in our house.

So I thought hard about making this monumental move. I thought about how the kids would take it, how my family would react, how long it would take to sell the house, how much packing there would be, how much it would cost to move, how tough it would be to start over. I didn't dwell on the why behind the move. I knew why. We needed a clean slate, and living in a faraway land seemed the perfect place to begin anew.

"Let's do it," I told Peter in early 1997. Almost immediately he found a buyer for *Tidewater Parent*, and the wheels began to turn. Before long, Peter and I found ourselves in the uncomfortable position of telling the women who worked for us that we were selling the magazine to the publishing company that owned *The Virginian-Pilot*, the region's daily paper.

"You can keep working for the magazine when the new owners take over," I said as cheerfully as I could in the sunny café where we were meeting.

Ronni, my sales rep, sat in stunned silence. Beth, my assistant editor, looked as if she'd been hit by a two-by-four. The waitress served our breakfast as we sat motionless.

"Why?" Ronni finally managed to squeak.

"Well, we're moving to Holland," I said. "We just need a change of scenery."

"Just call it the seven-year itch," Peter said with a chuckle. *Tidewater Parent* was exactly seven years old that summer.

"Gosh," Beth said, "I can't believe it. We'll miss you guys." I knew we would miss them, too, as well as the magazine that started so ominously the same month Sierra died. Her death and the launch of the magazine were all bound up in some inexplicable way. Maybe selling the business was another step we needed to take to move on to wherever it was we were going.

The weeks before we left to move to the Netherlands swam by in a crazy current. Selling our business in early June freed us to concentrate on the enormous task of moving our family and all our belongings across the ocean. First we had to get rid of a lot of junk we'd accumulated. Garage sales helped; giving stuff away did, too.

Yet we still found ourselves with 243 boxes of things we needed to take—or at least thought we needed: ceramic bowls, dinner plates, silverware, frying pans, building blocks, puzzles, bike helmets, soccer balls, warm coats, favorite sweaters, undershirts, scuffed-up shoes. Plus beds, dressers, our car, two computers, lamps, carpets, pillows, and tools—and boxes and boxes of more stuff.

Then there were the things we didn't necessarily need, but somehow couldn't live without: Peter's boyhood coin collection; old letters and notebooks from college; a dozen or so misshapen ceramic pots Scott and Jasper created in pottery class; my journals, detailing the seasons of my life; and stacks of photo albums, containing pictures of my parents when they were still together, my brothers before their hair turned gray, old boyfriends whose names I barely remembered, and Sierra.

Among the things I couldn't leave behind were a box of Sierra's clothes and the red shoes she barely had a chance to wear. I couldn't part with the small ceramic goose girl about four inches tall, painted in fairy-tale colors, and her lone white goose, which my brother Dick gave me when Sierra was born. Dick's wife, Nilla, told me then that Sierra was born on Goose Day, November 10, a traditional Swedish celebration to honor the girls who tended geese. Later I learned the Dutch also celebrate Goose Day.

The little goose had fallen to the floor once, breaking its long graceful neck, and Peter glued its head back on, leaving a thin scar to remind me that only some things in life are easy to put back together. After being repaired, the girl and her goose sat undisturbed on my dresser for many years until I packed them carefully in tissue paper and placed them in a small box to take their long journey across the ocean.

I knew that as soon as we found a place to live in the Netherlands, one of the first things I'd do would be to unwrap the goose girl and her little goose and place them carefully on my dresser again, a tangible reminder of the "Happily Ever After" ending I hoped Peter and I would find in our new life overseas.

My younger brother, Tom, threw us a farewell party a week before we left. In his backyard under the hot August sun, friends and family offered cheerful smiles and encouragement. Seven years had passed since Sierra died, and I wondered whether my family was getting better, staying the same, or if perhaps this bold move across the ocean was simply an escape, a chance to run away, to hide from the unfairness of life. Would we find what we were looking for? At Tom's party, I looked around at the smiling faces and wondered whether we were doing the right thing.

A scene played out in my mind. It was early August 1990, and a small blonde girl ran across our front yard, silhouetted by the evening sun's last rays. Sierra was saying goodbye as I drove off to a meeting.

Stretching her arm over her head, she waved to me, a gentle flowing wave—almost regal. I turned to watch her as I drove slowly down the road and waved back, feeling so loved and blessed to have Sierra as my daughter.

I began to realize how much a part of our family Sierra was and always would be. Her life and death led us here. Why? What could I learn from my daughter? What did she want me to know?

As Peter, our sons, and I prepared to embark on our new future in Europe, I felt as though a giant wave were poised to crash down on top of us. Now it was time to close our eyes, hold our breath, duck under, and swim like crazy to the other side.

Chapter 9

—⟨∾∾⟩—

Lingering sadness

A few days after arriving in the Netherlands, I called my mother on Peter's new cell phone to let her know the five of us had made it across the ocean safely.

It was September 1, 1997, and she was crying.

"What's wrong, Mom?"

"I'm watching them bring Princess Di's body home," she said, her voice crackling across the Atlantic from her home in Virginia.

"What did you say?" I shouted, standing in front of the bungalow we'd rented near Maastricht while we searched for a new home.

"Princess Diana," she said. "Her body is being brought back home to England. You heard about her accident, didn't you?"

"What accident?" I asked. Since arriving in the Netherlands a few days earlier, Peter and I had been focusing all of our energies on finding a place to live, registering our sons in school, and taking the many steps necessary to settle into this new land. Neither of us had watched the news or looked at a newspaper. We were suspended in time and space between our old life and our new one.

"She died, Peggy, yesterday," I heard my mom saying, her voice catching in her throat, "in a bad car accident in Paris."

Stunned, I immediately thought of Diana's two sons and how awful this must be for them, this terrible shattering event that would change their lives forever. Ever since Sierra died, I mourned the tragedies of others as though they were my own. I still couldn't listen to an ambulance siren without shuddering and remembering the wail of the ambulance the day Sierra died, a wail that echoed my own screams that endless afternoon, a wail that reverberated within me still, though it was softer now, gentler, and I had to stop and listen to hear it.

I still couldn't watch sad stories on television. I had to leave the room if something too terrible began to play out on the screen, even though no made-for-TV movie could ever match the drama that unfolded the day my daughter drowned. Yet seeing other people's anguish, even on TV, brought my own sorrow out of its hiding place, the spot where it was buried deep within. Princess Diana's death triggered the memories I tried so hard to keep locked away.

After saying goodbye to my mom, I walked to the playground, where Peter played with our sons, and I told them about Princess Di. When I finished, as if on cue, the sun disappeared behind a gray cloud, and a cool wind began to blow.

—◦◦◦—

Peter's mother, father, and sister joined us on the southern side of the Netherlands to help with the kids while Peter and I hunted for a place to live. They rented the bungalow next to ours and looked forward to enjoying a late summer vacation, but for Peter and me, there was no time to relax. We had only two weeks to find a home, and from what we'd heard, housing was a precious resource.

International business was exploding in Maastricht. The influx of foreign companies fed the local economy, boosting the price of housing, since newly arrived businessmen and their families brought huge sums of disposable income, most of it provided by their employers. The money paid for moving expenses, housing costs, new appliances, tuition for their children to attend the international school, even jazzy little cars for the mothers to zoom their kids to school in before joining the other international mothers for coffee or antique shopping just over the border in Belgium.

But Peter and I didn't have a large company footing the bill for our move or our rent or our children's tuition. As we began looking at housing costs in Maastricht and surrounding towns, both of us got sticker shock. Before leaving the U.S., we'd checked the Internet to see how much homes would cost in Maastricht, and while the real estate seemed pricey, we figured we could find more modest properties once we arrived. Now as we looked in the paper and talked to realtors, we realized living in the Netherlands was going to be more expensive than we thought.

"I told you," Peter's mother said as we gathered for dinner on a patio adjacent to their bungalow. "It costs much money to live here!" Jannie didn't speak English very well, and conversations with her were always short and to the point. "I think it costs not so much in Hoorn," Jannie continued. "Plenty of houses there for you."

Peter's family were ecstatic when he told them last spring that we were coming to live in the Netherlands, but his mom was decidedly nervous about our prospects since we didn't have jobs lined up or clear plans for the future. She wanted us to move nearer to Hoorn, a city north of Amsterdam where they lived, but Peter and I chose to settle a few hours away from his family, feeling that a little distance would be healthy for all of us.

The boys dashed off to the playground in the bungalow park, and Peter tried once again to explain to his mother why we chose to move to Maastricht. Peter spoke Dutch, of course, and I understood only part of what he said. He mentioned the better climate in the South: not as cold and windy as Hoorn. He talked about the ambience of the city of Maastricht, its history, its pastoral landscape, and the surrounding foothills—all of it more inviting than the flat cow pastures and canals up north. He reminded her of the excellent school the kids would attend.

He didn't tell her about the sliding fee scale at the international school, which meant the boys would get a private-school education at an affordable price since we fell into the lowest income range—at least until we started earning money.

He didn't tell her that both he and I felt that starting over in a strange land would bring us closer together. While my marriage to Peter seemed to be stable again, the lingering sadness of Sierra's death still got in the way. A change in scenery would, I hoped, help Peter and me focus more on our children and each other.

Maybe this whole move was my nod to Sierra, a way of acknowledging that her death gave me one thing at least: the wisdom to appreciate my family more, to give my children more time, more understanding, more attention. I wanted to be with them, to know them better, to love them more. Perhaps this was my way of trying to put my family back together, to create a new family, one that didn't have a hole in the middle where Sierra used to be. Leaving behind the place where sadness enveloped us—perhaps that was what we needed to heal.

—◦∞◦—

After days of driving and discussing and searching and hoping, Peter and I finally found a place to live: a three-story townhouse in a small village about ten minutes from Maastricht with four bedrooms, two bathrooms, and a playroom. Huge by Dutch standards, it cost only $850 per month. While not quite the cozy cottage in the countryside I'd envisioned, the townhouse had its good points, including a backyard with a small glass greenhouse and, even more important, a six-month lease. Since we planned to settle in the Netherlands for a few years, we wanted to buy a place—so a short-term rental was perfect.

Peter arranged for the container to be trucked in and hired a few guys to help unload our things. After unpacking a few boxes, we hopped into our Suburban, fresh out of the container, and drove into Maastricht to buy appliances. We needed a refrigerator, a TV, a washer and dryer, a vacuum cleaner, and a coffeemaker. The appliance store promised to deliver our purchases the next day, which was a good thing because laundry had been piling up ever since we arrived.

After hugs and kisses and promises to visit soon, Peter's sister and parents went back to Hoorn, to their lives up north. Now that we lived nearby, we would see more of Peter's family and, I hoped, grow closer: celebrating holidays and birthdays and getting to know each other better. The boys and I would start learning Dutch soon, so we could communicate better with Oma, Opa, and Tante Karin and learn about this new culture.

Scott, eleven, and Jasper, seven, seemed happy enough to be in the Netherlands. Not that they'd accepted this relocation without comment, but at their age, the boys still deferred to their parent's judgment, at least on the surface. We'd actually bribed them by buying a video game system they wanted—a peace offering, a way of thanking them for going along with us on our journey across the sea.

Now we were finally ready to unpack the Nintendo 64, and the kids were beside themselves. As Peter hooked everything up, we gathered in front of our American television, which we'd brought along expressly to use with the Nintendo. Scott and Jasper held tightly onto the controllers, thumbs poised, mouths open, waiting for Dad to plug in the converter and turn on the TV.

"O.K., here goes," Peter said, and for a moment the TV screen turned bright blue and then black again. A brief pop accompanied the blackness. Scott and Jasper looked at their father, somewhat confused, and then it dawned on them that something had gone seriously wrong.

Sheepishly Peter said, "Oops, guess I should have used a different converter. I think I fried the insides. It's probably worthless now." Jasper started to cry, unable to accept that his dad blew up the TV. Scott looked as if he wanted to cry, too, except he was too old to let the tears show.

I stood there thinking, That's a $250 TV set that Peter just ruined in about two seconds. Feeling myself becoming angry, I tried to control my emotions and said between clenched teeth, "Peter, I can't believe you used that dinky little converter on our practically brand-new TV. What were you thinking?"

Of course, I couldn't stay mad at Peter. A TV is just a box of metal with a tube, wires, and electrical circuits. It can be replaced. A relationship is a little more complex. Formed from bits and pieces of shared experiences, wired together with love, respect, and trust, a relationship is harder to fix if it blows up.

Chapter 10

—⟨ಌ⟩—

The nature of accidents

With the boys enrolled in the international school in Maastricht, life began to feel almost normal in the Netherlands. The challenging curriculum of the international school meant Scott faced a more intense school experience. Sixth grade was housed in the high school, and judging by the work Scott brought home, it seemed the subjects were high school level as well. Luckily, he didn't complain and spent his evenings up in his room, surrounded by books.

The first week I took two-year-old Ross to preschool, he cried every day. The second week he decided preschool was fine and walked in each morning with a huge grin on his face, joining the assortment of other kids from Denmark, France, Japan, and Great Britain. In charge of this motley group of preschoolers was Teacher Elsbeth, an attractive woman in her mid-twenties with black corkscrew curls and level gray eyes that probed beneath the surface.

Elsbeth started class each morning with her preschoolers seated around her in a tidy circle. Then she approached each one, saying, "Good morning, Emma (or Liam or Emile)." The child stood up, looked directly at Teacher Elsbeth, and said, "Good morning," while shaking hands firmly and competently. I'd never seen two- and three-year-olds shake hands with such aplomb. Elsbeth, who lived across the border in Belgium, had a cheery smile and a calm way about her that I appreciated. Ross liked her, too, and settled in nicely, eventually learning how to shake hands better than many grown-ups I know.

Not long after Ross started preschool, I told Elsbeth about Sierra. As the years had passed, I found it harder to tell people about my daughter. Sometimes it seemed Sierra was my big secret, which I held inside, unwilling to reveal to people I hardly knew. Other times, if a person were deserving enough, I opened up and shared my secret, as if I were relinquishing a fragile shell I'd found on the beach, one that became more precious when I gave it away.

The people in my life fell into two categories: those I met before Sierra died and those I met afterwards. A lucky few from the first group—my family and a few friends—actually knew Sierra when she was alive. It mattered so much to me when someone brought her up in conversation, recalled a memory. I felt sorry for the other group, those who never knew Sierra. In Maastricht no one knew about her unless I shared her story.

I informed Scott's and Jasper's teachers about Sierra, too, because they needed to know. That way they would understand if my sons hesitated when asked, "Do you have any sisters?" Scott still wasn't quite sure how to answer that question. At first he would say, "Yes, I had a sister named Sierra." He'd continue matter-of-factly, "She drowned." The questioner would invariably look pained and mumble something, leaving Scott feeling awkward and embarrassed. Eventually he started saying he only had two brothers.

I had the same problem. Should I tell or shouldn't I? Should I say I have three living children and one who's in heaven? Should I say I have three sons and omit Sierra from my answer, as though I were ashamed of her? I always felt I betrayed her memory when I didn't tell.

The telling was hard, though. When I confided in people, especially mothers, they often cried. Their eyes would fill up with tears as it dawned on them what I'd just said. Then I would feel odd because my eyes stayed dry. So I'd offer an excuse. "I cry sometimes in private" or "I've cried so much that the tears don't come as quickly as they used to." It was an awkward feeling to stand in front of someone who cried for your dead daughter and apologize for not weeping, too.

Elsbeth didn't show much emotion when I told her about Sierra. She just said, "I'm sorry to hear that," and accepted it without prying. That was the other problem with telling people. I felt as if I had to offer an explanation, a quick synopsis of an event that swirled in my memory like a tornado. "She drowned in my neighbor's pool when she was almost three" was my stock explanation. Then their tears would come, and I could only stammer and try to offer comfort.

※

Jasper, my especially sociable son, was welcomed as if he were the long-lost best friend of half the second graders at the international elementary school. He became instantly popular and received numerous invitations to sleep over and go to the movies and—this was the big one—eat at McDonalds on Wednesdays after school. Unfortunately, his prim and proper British teacher, Mrs. Clark, didn't find Jasper quite so endearing. One day a note came home from school about Jasper using the f-word.

"The f-word?" I said to Peter in genuine surprise and made an appointment with Mrs. Clark.

A few days later we sat facing each other in child-sized chairs in her cluttered classroom.

"Jasper is a little low," Mrs. Clark began in her clipped British accent, pointy glasses perched on her nose, her face framed by greasy bangs and straight gray hair.

"What do you mean?" I responded, a hint of defensiveness in my voice. "He's always done fine in school. He's smart for his age.

In fact, he's older than most kids in his class."

Mrs. Clark's patronizing response followed, "Yes, well, I know that. I am also aware that he is emotionally older than the others. Let me show you what I mean."

She showed me a drawing Jasper made of a stick figure with two arms, two legs, fingers, and curly hair. It was a boy with a pierced earring and something hanging from his left nostril.

Mrs. Clark nodded sagely and said, "Yes, he is quite mature for his age," and she showed me pictures her other students had drawn, and none of them had earrings or boogers coming from their noses. Then Mrs. Clark pursed her lips and began showing me his papers, and I listened with dismay to words like "dreadful handwriting" and "sloppy reading skills." I thought about my dreams for my sons' academic success and wondered whether moving my children halfway around the world was a mistake.

—⁓—

One day during our first month in the Netherlands, something happened that made me realize it doesn't matter where you live or what you do to avoid it, danger is always at your doorstep.

Peter and I sat in our living room with Ross, poring over the real estate section of the newspaper when Scott rushed through the front door, saying, "Jasper's been in an accident. He's bleeding. He's hurt bad."

Peter grabbed his car keys. "Where is he?" he demanded.

Scott said, "On the steep hill," and Peter was gone, the door slamming behind him.

I looked at Scott, my heart beating so hard I could hear it. "What happened?"

"We were riding our bikes down the steep hill," he explained, crying and trying to catch his breath, "and Jasper went too fast and lost control. He fell off his bike. I think he knocked some of his teeth out."

The steep hill? Not the incredibly steep hill two streets back that any sane person knew not to ride a bike down, much less ride a bike down trying to go fast. Some of his teeth out? He knocked some of his teeth out? Oh God, not his big, gorgeous, perfect, new permanent front teeth that had just barely finished coming in.

Scott stood there, upset, looking at me. "Should I go back there?"

I nodded, and he ran out the door, leaving me with Ross in the quiet living room, my thoughts swirling. Not another accident. Please God, not another accident. Suddenly I thought, "What am I doing here?" and buckled Ross in the stroller and ran out the door towards the steep hill.

A well-dressed old man wearing a hat walked toward me on the other side of the street, and I said—in English because I was too distraught to attempt Dutch—"The accident. Were you there? Is he all right?"

He pointed to his teeth, shook his head, and held up three or four fingers.

My mouth dropped open, and I said, "Bedankt," having remembered how to say thank you in Dutch at least. I kept running, pushing Ross in the stroller, and at the end of the street I saw our blue-and-white Suburban pass by in a blur. Seconds later it appeared again, and I ran up to it and looked in the back seat, where Jasper sat, crying, his face all scraped up, his mouth open. I saw a black space where a front tooth used to be. My son looked like the Abominable Snowman in "Rudolph, the Red-Nosed Reindeer," except in the TV show, there was no blood, and now blood streamed down Jasper's face, mixing with tears, staining his clothes and the seat of the car. Scott sat next to his little brother, crying, too.

Peter said, "He knocked out a tooth."

"Just one?" I asked. "Thank God. Where is it?"

"Some doctor who lives on this street washed it off."

"Where is it?" I'd heard that a tooth could be replanted, but it needed to be placed in the mouth or in milk immediately for best results. Jasper found the tooth on the seat, and I told him to put it in his mouth.

"Don't swallow it," I said. I wanted to hug him and comfort him because he was crying hard and in pain, but they had to hurry off to the emergency room at the hospital. As they drove away, leaving Ross and me standing on the sidewalk, I saw a big dent in the side of the Suburban and wondered what had happened.

Walking up the hill, I found blood on the street and stood there, tearful and lost. A woman came out of her house and said she saw the boys seconds before the accident, racing downhill in a blur. Then she told me her own son, who's now twenty, crashed into a car at the bottom of the hill while on his bike and was in a coma for a long time and never fully recovered.

I realized how easily Jasper could have been killed if a car had backed out of a driveway while he was going full-tilt down the hill. Suddenly I found myself telling this total stranger about Sierra, and I cried even harder. The woman invited me in, but I wanted to go home and wait for word from Peter, so I thanked her anyway. We hugged and said goodbye, and I never saw her again.

Later that night Peter told me about crashing into a brick wall while hurrying to find Jasper; about rushing into the emergency room at the hospital in Maastricht, Jasper covered in blood and crying, and the receptionist telling him, "Sorry dental emergencies aren't handled here. You must go to the other side of the highway"; about getting back in the car, careening across the highway to the designated office building, where the dentist, knowing how important each passing minute was, rushed Jasper in to replant the chipped, broken tooth. The dentist told Peter that Jasper's other front tooth was also damaged and would probably die.

That day I learned a lesson: to find out first thing where to obtain emergency medical and dental assistance in any new place. It seems obvious, doesn't it? I thought back to Sierra's accident and the guilt that plagued me still because I hadn't watched her that day. And now Jasper could easily have been killed because I'd let him ride his bike with only his big brother to watch him, believing he could handle the freedom. Both times I failed my children.

I found myself wondering about the nature of accidents. Since Sierra died, I'd spoken with so many parents who admitted sometimes when they turned their backs for a moment, their kids had narrowly escaped tragic accidents. During a visit to England, my friend Lauren was washing dishes when her three-year-old son, Ian, wandered out of her parents' front door and down a busy sidewalk just steps away from a road full of speeding cars. But Lauren dashed after him and caught him before he toddled into the street.

Why do accidents happen? Why do some soldiers die in battle and others come back safely? Why do some teenagers get hurt in car accidents and others walk away? All I know is that every parent of every child who dies feels responsible somehow, as though we have failed in our most important mission.

Chapter 11

—❧—

Like aimless clouds

We settled into an easy routine that fall in Maastricht and even organized a carpool with an Austrian mom, Katharina, who lived nearby and whose son, Constantin, became Jasper's best friend. Peter and I took turns each morning, ferrying Constantin, his sister Caroline, Scott, Jasper, and Ross to the international school. At noon, I picked up Ross; then at three Katharina brought the older children home.

Some days when Katharina couldn't pick up Scott and Jasper, they caught the bus home—that is, unless they missed it. On those days, I sat in our townhouse and watched the clock, worrying about all the things that could go wrong when an eleven-year-old and a seven-year-old try to catch a bus home. Invariably, the phone rang, and Scott would say, "Mom, we missed the bus," or "Mom, the bus didn't stop for us." And I'd buckle Ross into the car and make my third run of the day to the international school, weaving through narrow, bicycle-filled streets in our oversized Suburban, getting back home as dusk fell and another day of our new life in Europe faded into night.

While the kids were in school, Peter and I explored nearby villages and discussed where to live and what kind of work to do. We searched tirelessly for a house to call home, a cozy brick cottage with red geraniums spilling from the windowsills, dark green shutters framing lace-draped windows, and a small yard with enough room for a garden and a swing set. We scoured the newspapers and the countryside, checking out places for sale. Most of the time the asking prices seemed ridiculously high, considering the houses were so much smaller than homes in Virginia Beach.

Our old house was still on the market. The agent assured us via email that she was showing it regularly, but we weren't getting any offers. Peter originally suggested staying in Virginia Beach until we sold the house, but I wanted the kids to start the school year on time. Of course, we were disappointed that the house wasn't selling, especially since we were sending a mortgage payment back to the U.S. each month, in addition to paying rent on our townhouse.

When I considered the money we'd spent so far on this move— our plane tickets, health insurance, moving expenses, the cost of renting a car for three weeks until we could get ours out of the container, rent for the vacation bungalow and for the townhouse, school tuition, new appliances, the money we spent on gas for the Suburban, groceries, the Internet, phone, natural gas, electricity, new clothes for school, and of course the dentist bills—I was afraid to add it all up. Peter was in charge of our finances, and I tried not to think about our savings dwindling away.

We began to feel a sense of urgency about making an income. The trouble was, even though we spent hours discussing what kind of business to start, we couldn't seem to agree on what to do. Katharina, whose husband worked for KNP, a large paper company, suggested we start a relocation business. "You can work for international companies, helping new hires settle in the area," she said.

Peter and I decided that sounded like a good idea and started a database of international businesses. We designed business cards and a brochure and chose to call our company Star Relocation Services, naming it after the symbol for the city of Maastricht. Peter set up a database of real estate properties, and that's when our plan came to an abrupt halt. A housing shortage in the Netherlands was especially severe in the Maastricht region, and when Peter approached local real estate professionals, they wouldn't reveal their listings. With a sigh, we filed away our brochures and business cards and tried to come up with other ideas for making money.

Like aimless clouds, the days floated by.

—◦◦◦—

"What about publishing?" I suggested to Peter one afternoon in our home office in Maastricht. "It worked for us in the U.S. Why not here?"

Peter didn't respond.

"What about a magazine in English called *International Family*?" I asked. "We could distribute it through the international schools. I think we can find advertisers for it, don't you, Peter?"

After a moment, Peter said, "Maybe." He didn't seem very enthusiastic. Forging ahead, I designed new business cards, started a list of international schools, and set up a database of companies that might like to sponsor this new family magazine. Next I began brainstorming potential advertisers: banks, furniture stores, moving companies, appliance chains, travel destinations, car dealerships, and retail stores.

I planned editorial content for the first issue, including an article about finding a dentist in your new city as soon as you arrive. Other ideas for articles sprang forth in my mind faster than I could jot them down because everything Peter, our children, and I were experiencing as we adjusted to life in the Netherlands was fodder for articles for other expatriate families.

The headmaster at the international school said, "Great idea! Sure, you can distribute your magazine in my school." Then he invited me to The Hague in November for a conference, where he would introduce me to headmasters from other Dutch international schools. "I'm sure they'll like your idea," he said.

Peter and I started shopping for a printing company and discovered we'd have to pay extra to transform our layout boards into computerized files. This step added significantly to the cost of producing the magazine, but was required by all the printing companies we contacted. Next we found out how much paper cost in the Netherlands, double what it cost in the U.S., and our business plan took another punch. Then Peter started calling up banks, furniture stores, and big grocery chains, and no one seemed interested in our wonderful new magazine. I started thinking, "Is this another mistake?" And discouragement seeped into our lives.

A pall settled over our narrow townhouse with too many walls and not enough windows, which we began referring to as the Cave. I still dreamed of the bright, cozy cottage that lingered like a painting in my thoughts, but the vision was fading around the edges.

It's not that Maastricht was such a bad place to live. In our small village there was a market every Thursday in the town square, where I shopped for vegetables and fruit. Next to the square was a park, where I strolled with Ross in the afternoons past a pond full of ducks and swans. And from morning to night, as if to remind us of the passing of time, the towering cathedral in the center of town rang its melancholy bells across the rooftops of the village and over the fields beyond.

The days grew shorter as autumn drifted by. And though the weather was crisp and clear, the landscape golden, the countryside like a postcard, we barely noticed, absorbed by our gloomy thoughts. We didn't like where we lived, our business ideas seemed doomed to fail, and our bank balance dropped precipitously each month. Peter's discontent grew daily, I started smoking again, and our discussions about the future became more heated. Meanwhile, we were still taking our kids to school every day, still putting up a brave front for our new international friends.

Occasionally the facade crumbled, however, as it did one night when we joined the parents' group from Scott's school for dinner at a tiny Italian restaurant near the riverfront in the oldest neighborhood in Maastricht. On a cool night in early November, Peter and I donned our best evening attire, left the kids with a babysitter, and found ourselves mingling with a sophisticated crowd of thirty or so international adults in a crowded candle-lit restaurant.

I jumped right into the throng, greeting familiar faces and introducing myself to unfamiliar ones. After Peter and I found a seat at the long table, waiters began taking orders, a lengthy process with such a large group. But there was plenty of conversation, and red wine flowed freely from straw-covered bottles. After awhile, talk turned to the slow service and growing hunger pangs. I noticed Peter was slurring his words, becoming slightly belligerent, actually getting angry because he was hungry and had drunk too much wine.

When the food finally came, Peter was over the edge. I began eating, but Peter didn't touch his food. Instead, he started calling the Italian owner "Stupido" and mumbled disparaging remarks about Italians in general. I looked around at these well-dressed people, whose circles I wanted to join. Then I looked at Peter, who was growing increasingly hostile. The others acted polite about Peter's condition and pretended not to notice how drunk he'd become, but I was mortified. I coaxed him out of the restaurant before he and the owner started rolling up their shirtsleeves, and we walked in silence to the car, our footsteps echoing in the empty street. Driving home, I wondered how I could ever face those people again. In my heart I knew that Peter's unhappiness was affecting him in more and more obvious ways.

It became evident when he tried to sell advertising for *International Family* and couldn't find any buyers. It was there when we looked for a new place to live, when we filled up the gas tank, paid the bills, watched our money disappear, and wondered where all this was leading.

Even though things weren't going as planned, we decided to buy a roomy camper for weekend trips to explore nearby villages and towns. During autumn break we headed to Germany's Mosel River region, where we forgot our troubles long enough to relax and savor our surroundings. We tasted wines, munched fat sausages, climbed mountains, and watched smiling Germans stomp grapes in their bare feet. After a much-needed break from our worrisome routine, we returned to Maastricht, refreshed and ready to go to work. Trouble was we still hadn't figured out what we wanted to do.

———∽∽∽———

One evening at dinner Peter said he just couldn't work from our townhouse anymore—too many distractions. I wondered if he meant me. He found a tiny office in the city with big windows for $1000 a month, not bad for a classy location in the heart of Maastricht. Peter bought new office furniture, a copy machine, and a dress coat because the weather was turning cold. He wore his nice suit and tie and coat and went to work every day and planned things and made calls and spent money, but nothing that he did or I did seemed destined to succeed.

We made an appointment with the director of Maastricht's economic development office to see whether he might be interested in supporting our new magazine. On the designated day, wearing our best clothes, Peter in his new coat and I in my high heels, we met Jacques, a wound-up, wiry Dutchman whose pointy nose and beady eyes reminded me of a hungry hawk. He ushered us into his sleek office in a richly renovated historic building in the center of Maastricht.

In our hands we carried a proposal in which we invited the city of Maastricht to become a sponsor of *International Family*. This magazine would be the perfect vehicle to spread the word about this wonderful city to the international community scattered across the Netherlands, we explained to Jacques, brimming with enthusiasm, and then offered a full-color advertisement on the back page as part of the package, all for a very reasonable price.

Time stood still as Peter and I waited for Jacques' reaction, the fate of *International Family* hanging in mid-air. Suddenly we heard a kind of exploding sound between Jacques' pursed lips. It was the sound you'd make if you blew up a balloon and suddenly the balloon was no longer there. Stunned, Peter and I watched Jacques start giggling, clear his throat, then tell us that the economic development office of the city of Maastricht was not in the business of giving away money.

"But—" Peter and I said in unison, trying vainly to explain that the city would get something back for its investment: visibility and exposure throughout the Netherlands. Jacques made it clear, however, as he ushered us out the door, that the development office didn't have the slightest interest in participating in our business venture. Somehow Peter and I stumbled out onto the street after shaking hands with Jacques. "Good luck!" he called after us, and we got the feeling he didn't really mean what he said.

As we walked through the center of Maastricht, Peter and I took turns imitating the PPPTTTT sound Jacques made. We laughed and said, "How unprofessional he was," but then we stopped laughing and grew quiet, lost in our private thoughts, afraid to admit that something was terribly wrong.

Chapter 12

—ᴄᴠᴏ—

An empty landscape

Is our sin one of carelessness? I asked myself as I sat smoking in the kitchen of our townhouse one morning while everyone still slept. Is it hubris? Are Peter and I too self-absorbed to be good parents, to succeed in business, to live satisfying lives? This move overseas was supposed to bring us closer together, but it felt as if the gulf separating Peter and me were growing larger. I sensed he didn't want to stay in the Netherlands, although he hadn't admitted it. He knew how badly I wanted this move to work out for us, how desperately I needed something good to happen.

Nearly every day I came face to face with little Dutch girls who reminded me of Sierra—blonde, blue-eyed, round-faced. I saw them in playgrounds, at school, in grocery stores—but they weren't Sierra. She wasn't here.

Suddenly everything felt wrong. It was almost as if Sierra's death brought about a curse. Maybe moving here had been a mistake. Maybe we were looking for answers in the wrong places. We were definitely not happier living here. In fact, things seemed to be getting worse. Two and a half months remained on the lease for our house, and Peter's office lease stretched even longer. We were depleting our savings on ordinary living expenses, and there was no money coming in. Peter grew more negative with each passing day.

One day I told Peter I'd found a lovely, large country house for rent, and we made an appointment to see it. I fell in love with the spacious home surrounded by woods and fields only about five minutes from Maastricht. But the rent was high, and the landlord required a two-year lease. In addition, the huge, drafty house probably cost a fortune to heat, and Peter said, "Peggy, it's just not worth it."

"But what else is there to do?" I asked. "Go back to Virginia? I'll feel like such a failure. Besides we haven't tried hard enough. Maybe we should get jobs." And for Peter, who has always been his own boss, getting a job was almost as bad as going on the dole. I persisted, so Peter set out for the employment agencies to see what was available. I came along, too, but not being fluent in Dutch meant my chances of finding work were minimal.

We found job openings two and a half hours away in Amsterdam, but did we want to uproot ourselves again just to get a job in an even more crowded city? Hardly any housing was available in Amsterdam, and it was even more expensive than in Maastricht. Finally, Peter, his head hanging lower as November turned into December, said, "There are no jobs here for me," which really meant he'd rather do almost anything than work for a boss.

Still I was reluctant to give up. "Let's wait a bit longer," I said, "before we make any rash decisions." Katharina told me that her husband was looking for someone to do the KNP international newsletter, written in English and distributed all over the world. "I can do that," I told Peter.

Michael, Katharina's husband, said, "Send me your resumé." And I thought, "Here's the break we need." Then Michael said KNP would donate the paper for the first issue of *International Family*.

"See, Peter, it can work," I said, trying to sound convincing. "It will work. We'll find a nice place to live. The kids are getting adjusted to school, and I'm making new friends. Peter? Peter?" But he wasn't showing any enthusiasm, so I began to lose mine. Why should I pursue a job or a business venture when Peter seemed to be withdrawing more and more? Every day he left for his office in town, but I didn't know what he was doing or thinking—except I knew he didn't share my vision for the future.

Now and then during those December days we escaped the Cave to walk on winding roads past idyllic homes and farms that blended with the scenery, just like in my painting. Pushing Ross in the stroller, Scott and Jasper trailing behind, we passed fruit orchards and rushing streams, grazing horses and tall woods, rustic farms and cozy courtyards with old wooden carts and farm tools and flowerpots full of purple and yellow pansies, postcard-perfect scenes of rural Dutch life.

But none of these places was ever for sale, much less for rent, and even if they were, the prices would be prohibitive. Like a fading mirage, my dream of finding happiness abroad was disintegrating before my eyes. In its place an empty landscape loomed.

———⁕———

Peter and I sat in the glass greenhouse in our backyard and discussed everything endlessly, analyzing each move we'd made, reliving the mistakes. We chastised ourselves for being so foolish, for spending vast sums of money and having nothing to show for it.

I began to see that my marriage to Peter was more important than my stubborn dream of living in Europe; that it didn't matter what kind of house we lived in or what kind of business we started, Peter wasn't happy in the Netherlands and never would be. Neither of us had predicted that he would feel so adamantly opposed to living in the country of his birth.

It was time to go.

I felt as though I had failed somehow. How could I ever look someone in the face again and say, "Listen to your heart. Go after your dreams."? Giving up was like losing Sierra all over again.

When she died, so did my dream of a normal life. Now my dream of living in Europe, my brave attempt to get back the happiness I'd once known, was ebbing away like a retreating tide. I mourned the loss of this dream, just as I'd mourned the loss of my normal life seven years before.

What would I say to my new friends at the international school? To Elsbeth, who'd become a confidant, or Katharina? How could I admit we were leaving, that this move had been a mistake, that we'd been wrong to try to make a go of it in a strange place with no job and few prospects?

How could I face the headmaster and say we weren't going to publish *International Family* after all? And what about those parents from the international school who listened so avidly when I told them about our new magazine and who agreed it was a great idea, bound to work, and they couldn't wait to read it? What would we say to Scott and Jasper and Ross, who were just beginning to feel at home in this new land, making friends, playing soccer on the village teams, finally getting the hang of riding the bus home once or twice a week?

And what would we do about the two-year lease Peter signed on his office? And what about all these appliances we bought? And the big question remained—Where would we go? Would we get another container and reload all our stuff and send it sailing across the ocean again, following with our tails between our legs? Would we go back to the city we left behind? Would we go backwards?

Peter knew where to go. He said the magic word one cold, stormy night in mid-December as we sat in the greenhouse. Upstairs our sons slept in their beds, blissfully unaware that their little lives were about to turn upside down again.

"Travel," Peter said. "We could just travel."

Actually, we had discussed this idea a year before when we first considered moving to Europe. Peter said then, "Maybe we should just travel for a few months in Europe. Leave all our stuff behind. Then we can look for a place we like and try it out before we move there."

Of course, in retrospect his words made incredibly good sense, but being sensible was never my strong suit. In fact, the most sensible thing to do right now would be to hightail it back to the U.S., where we knew how to start a business or get a job, where the living would be easy. Anything would be easier than what we'd been going through during this strange interlude in our lives, this chapter that was drawing slowly, inexorably to a close.

On the other hand, traveling sounded like the finest plan we'd had in a long, long time. I thought about that roomy camper we bought, the one we christened on our trip to Germany, waiting for us to climb aboard and take off. We could do it. It was within our grasp. I could homeschool the kids, and we could travel through Europe for six months or more if we liked it and really wanted to go for broke.

The candlelight flickered as the wind came through a crack in the garden house. I said, "O.K. Let's do it. Let's travel through Europe."

The rain drummed a beat on the glass roof. Peter and I smiled. We were ready to move on.

———

On the way home from school on a cloudy December afternoon, the boys and I stopped at a farm to buy a Christmas tree. Together we chose a small one and looked for someone to pay. I still felt awkward speaking Dutch, and even after being in the Netherlands four months, I always asked, "Sprecht U engels?" The woman shook her head, so I searched for the correct words to carry out the transaction.

"Hoe veel kost die boom?"

"Twintig guilden."

"Goed. Ik zal die boom nemen."

I found twenty guilders in my wallet, paid the lady, and we slid the tree into the back of the Suburban. The boys and I climbed in, and we drove home through the dusky pink twilight. I still couldn't get used to the amazingly short winter days.

That evening as we decorated the tree, Peter and I announced our plan to take the family on an extended camping trip. Scott and Jasper had grown comfortable with our new life in Maastricht, and we weren't sure how they'd feel about taking off for six months to strange, faraway places.

"Boys, how would you like to take a long vacation in the camper?" Peter said.

"You mean next summer?" Scott asked.

"No, sooner than that," Peter answered.

"As soon as we can get ready to go," I added. "Probably in February."

"Where to?" Jasper asked. "For how long?"

"Well, we plan to travel about six months, but we haven't worked out exactly where yet," Peter said. "Definitely south where it's warm."

Neither Scott nor Jasper asked why were leaving, a question I wasn't even sure I could answer. Were we leaving because we couldn't make things work here? Was it because we still felt Sierra's loss so strongly? Were we just running away from the sadness in our lives again? Had this move to Europe been a mistake? Or was it a stepping stone to the place we needed to be?

Scott and Jasper looked confused. No wonder. How could they feel confident in their future when Peter and I were so uncertain about ours? We watched them processing this news and waited for their reaction.

Suddenly a big grin spread across Jasper's face, and he said, "Does that mean we don't have to go to school?"

"Well," I answered. "You won't go to school, but we will have lessons in the camper."

"You mean, we'll be homeschooled?" asked Scott.

"That's right," I said. "It'll be fun. We'll study Ancient Greece and Rome and then be able to see the places we learn about."

"Will school last all day?" Jasper asked.

"Nope, that's the good part," I explained. "We'll only have school about two or three hours a day, maybe just three days a week. The rest of the time we'll be sightseeing, going to museums and places like that."

"What about kids to play with?" Scott asked.

"Well, you always have your brothers to play with," I answered. "Plus you'll meet kids at the campgrounds where we stay and you'll get to spend a lot of time with your dad and me!"

Neither Scott nor Jasper looked too enthusiastic about this last revelation.

"Where will we go when the trip's over?" asked Jasper.

I looked at Peter. After a pause, he said, "We're not exactly sure, but there's a possibility we'll go back to Virginia Beach."

"Yaaayyy!" Jasper shouted and jumped up with glee. He still missed his friends from our old neighborhood. "Let's go!"

Scott had a big grin on his face, too. Even Ross, who at age two wasn't quite comprehending everything, looked happy. Suddenly it hit me that Peter's and my gloomy dispositions had affected the whole family, but we'd been so caught up in our own angst, we hadn't noticed. These poor kids of ours were playing along, but in reality, Maastricht wasn't where they wanted to be either.

Chapter 13

—⟊⟊—

A collision course with the universe

As 1998 dawned, Peter and I began planning our six-month camping adventure. Sitting over coffee in the morning, shopping in the grocery store, or relaxing with a bottle of wine at the end of the day, we talked nonstop about all the details involved in leaving Maastricht and embarking on this long journey.

We discussed logistics: what to do with our furniture and the Volvo I recently purchased. We contemplated where to go on our trip, which countries to visit, which ones to skip. We made lists of household items to bring, supplies to buy, books for homeschooling.

We decided to depart the end of February when the lease was up on our townhouse. Peter decided it was safe to renege on the lease for his office space in Maastricht since he'd done a number of improvements to the property. I worried about legal ramifications, but Peter assured me everything would be fine, and I decided to believe him.

The dynamics of my relationship with Peter seemed to be entering a new phase. I found myself relying more heavily on him now. Peter was always a strong, take-charge type, but I too could be strong-willed. We were both persuasive but over the years had maintained a good balance between what he wanted and what I wanted. As we began to make plans for this six-month odyssey through Europe, however, I found myself falling into a more submissive role.

That's not to say I didn't contribute to the decisions we made, but I submitted to Peter more and more frequently. Perhaps it was because I felt tired of making decisions, tired of watching our family roll like a tumbleweed over the desert sands, tired of wondering whether the choices I'd made had sent that weed spinning off on a collision course with the universe.

Peter and I shared a mixture of excitement and anxiety over our impending trip. It was a happy occasion. Who wouldn't love to take six months off from the real world to explore exotic landscapes, see ancient history come to life, relax on sunny beaches, and best of all not work?

Yet beneath the excitement and anticipation was an undercurrent of worry. Where in the world would we end up?

—◦◦◦—

Staff at international schools, used to a lot of coming and going, took the news of our impending departure in stride. Jasper's class made a Goodbye Book, in which his classmates drew pictures and wrote comments, such as "Have a safe trip!" and "Nice knowing you!" When Jasper brought it home, he didn't seem too excited about it, but I looked at every page.

A few mothers from the international school invited me for a farewell lunch. We met at De Kadans, one of my favorite restaurants in Maastricht. Nestled beside the Maas River, De Kadans was a cozy place with wooden floors, round tables, good food, and efficient waiters.

The women were all cheerful and friendly, but as I sat with

them and made small talk, I realized how different we were. Unlike me, these women hadn't chosen to come to Maastricht; instead they'd followed their husbands here. I found myself somewhat envious of these ladies whose lives seemed to be all laid out for them. Peter and I had to make choices about which direction to take.

I learned that the fewer choices you have to make, the easier life is to navigate. Peter and I had spilled buckets of energy throughout our years together, trying to figure out what to do. While some may think that having choices and being able to change the direction of your life is a luxury, it can also be a frightening responsibility.

It's true that some folks are so caught up in lives that have swallowed them whole, they haven't got the energy to escape. They let life happen to them instead of the other way around. I thought back to when Peter and I first announced our move to Europe. Many of our friends had said, "What courage you have to follow your dreams, to invent your lives." At the time, we glowed with pride and smiled, believing we were creating a better life for ourselves and our children.

Things looked different now as I sat with these mothers in the restaurant, eating our salads, smiling and chatting. Though they didn't ask too many questions, they knew Peter's and my attempt to find a new life in this place hadn't been successful. Rather than look back at the past, however, they asked what was ahead.

"Where will you go?" one mother wondered.

"Well, we're heading south where the weather's better!" I answered.

Everyone laughed because February in the Netherlands is downright cold and gloomy.

"Got room in your trunk?" another mother asked.

I could tell the women were awed by our plans to travel for six months. Unlike our enthusiastic move to Maastricht half a year before, however, I had mixed feelings about this trip. I felt so worn out from trying to make a go of it here, I didn't really know what to think.

The mothers and I said goodbye to each other in front of the restaurant as the wind whipped our hair. "Send postcards," they called. "Come back and visit."

"I will," I said, smiling, but in my heart I knew I would never see them again.

———ﾟﾟﾟ———

Near the end of February, preparations began for Maastricht's Carnival. Residents of Limburg, a largely Roman Catholic province, threw a big party right before the start of the Lenten season, as do many Catholic populations around the world. Carnival in Maastricht was a three-day affair with parades, marching bands, colorful costumes, and beer, lots and lots of beer. In my mind, I pictured it as a splashy send off, a happy ending to a chapter in our lives that hadn't been especially joyful.

The day before Ash Wednesday, Peter, the boys, and I drove into the city. Looking around, we saw that nearly everyone was in costume, drinking beer, and celebrating. In our regular clothes, we felt like outsiders. Peter bought a couple of beers, and we listened to a band play on a street corner, trying to join in the spirit of the festive crowd. Before long the kids began to complain about the cold and pester us to take them home.

Peter took a few photos, and we managed feeble smiles, but there was something overwhelmingly sad about being there. We didn't fit in. We tried to blend into the culture of this country, to go Dutch, but it hadn't worked. Standing on the streets of Maastricht, we watched the parade march right past us and realized this chapter was over.

After six months of trying to begin new lives in the Netherlands, Peter and I felt emptier than ever. Maastricht offered us no magic answers. It was, after all, just geography, just a place whose meaning was rooted in the experiences of those who lived in its boundaries. Ever since our arrival, the days and weeks had been clouded by a longing we couldn't really name. Changing the scenery hadn't helped us elude the sadness in our lives.

Even now the sadness lingered over us. It hovered as Peter, the boys, and I walked through the merry Carnival crowds, past the marching bands and crazy costumes, the decorated storefronts, the smiling faces. It followed us as we wandered back to our car, as we drove to our townhouse, as we ate our dinner and wondered whether we'd ever find a place that felt like home.

Traveling for the next six months was a way to put off that sinking feeling we'd had ever since Sierra died—the sense that the peace we craved would always lurk just over the horizon. We could only hope that at the end of this journey, we'd catch up with it somewhere.

—◆◆◆—

Peter and I packed nearly every day. Putting our things back into boxes so soon after unpacking them felt wrong somehow. To look at the mountains of toys, books, household items, clothes, and accoutrements of life and consider how little we used most of these things made me shake my head. We had tried to downsize when we left Virginia and did in fact get rid of a lot. But we were still buried under huge snowdrifts of junk. Of course, having three busy boys with toys, books, and games was part of the problem, but Peter and I tended to be pack rats, too.

Everything went into two piles: one pile would be packed up and put into storage while we traveled, and the other pile included things we'd bring along on our six-month journey. Each item we owned needed to go through a litmus test as Peter and I pondered whether it was necessary for our trip or could be relegated to the storage heap.

We planned to follow the coastline on our camping journey. After cruising south through Luxembourg and Germany, we would stop in Switzerland to see an old friend, then scoot down to Italy, follow the east coast southward, cross by ferry to Greece, circle the shores of the Peloponnese before ferrying back to Italy, heading up the west coast, veering westward through France, then around Spain's circumference to Portugal, and back up to France's west coast. Then we guessed our time would be up, and we'd begin preparing to leave Europe behind. I liked the symbolism of cruising along the coasts. We'd be traveling on the edge—caught between our old lives and the new ones just beyond the horizon.

Our camper, dubbed The Coaster, was large—about thirty feet long—with tons of storage space, and I was determined to fill it all. An amazing number of books, for example, fell into the trip pile: homeschooling books and binders filled with lesson plans I'd purchased, as well as assorted guides to help us navigate the countries we'd be visiting.

Besides bulky books, items we'd need on the road included a new "voortent"—an add-on room that attached to the camper, a roll of indoor/outdoor carpet, folding table and chairs, charcoal grill, gas cooker, clothes spinner, tools, extension cords, lanterns, coolers, buckets, cleaning supplies, laundry baskets, coffee maker, laptop, and toaster. We also needed toys, bicycles, sleeping bags, pillows, winter clothes, summer clothes, plates, pots and pans, coffee mugs, wine glasses, television, radio, coats, jackets, port-a-potty, maps, food, trash can, diapers, first-aid kit, and my personal must-have kitchen items: a salad spinner, corkscrew, and olive pitter.

These things went into our trip pile—while the furniture, stereo, computers, file cabinets, knick-knacks, photo albums, paintings, vases, blankets, curtains, and boxes that we never got around to unpacking went into our storage pile. Included in this group was my ceramic goose girl and her little white goose with the crack around its neck. I wondered when I'd see them again—and where their next home would be. In the meantime, they were destined to sit in a box in a dark corner of a warehouse along with all of our other things until we came back to claim them sometime in the hazy future.

The day before we were to depart, Peter parked the camper up the hill from our townhouse, the closest he could get because there were no parking spaces out front. All five of us, even little Ross, hiked up the hill dozens of times, carrying the gear we needed for our six-month journey. The storage spaces in the camper filled up quickly, so we found creative places to store things, such as the shower stall in our tiny bathroom, where we piled in the cleaning supplies, the laundry basket, and the clothes spinner. Under the beds we stored roller blades, Legos, and books. The last thing we did was strap our bikes onto the back of the Suburban. We were finally ready to roll.

Tonight we would sleep in our townhouse for the last time. Tired from all the moving and carrying and loading we'd done, the boys zonked out in their beds, and Peter and I visited the glass greenhouse one more time.

"Well, what d'ya think, Peg?" Peter said as he settled on the sandy floor, a beer in one hand and a candle in the other. I was smoking what I decided would be my last cigarette.

"I'm ready to go," I answered. "We tried to make it work here, but somehow I think this just wasn't the place for us."

"Yeah, I know," Peter said softly. "I'm sorry it didn't work out. I know you really had your heart set on living here."

"It's O.K., Peter. I don't mind that we're leaving. I like the idea of being untethered for a few months. Who wouldn't?" I smiled. "Besides we get to hide from the real world a little longer. I like that."

Peter and I sat in silence and listened to the wind blow outside. Above in the night sky, yellow stars—like a thousand eyes—looked down at us in our little glass house. They blinked down at the boys asleep in their bunk beds upstairs. They sparkled down on our townhouse with too many walls and not enough windows, on our little village near the city of Maastricht, on the province of Limburg, on the country called the Netherlands, on the continent of Europe, on the Western Hemisphere, on the whole wide world. Like silent sentries, the stars stood watch over all of us that night.

Peter and I looked up at them, hoping perhaps to see answers written there in the sky. But the stars said nothing; they just blinked as if to acknowledge that they too were waiting.

Suddenly, one star shot sideways across the sky, and I shivered. It was Sierra, my shooting star, and she was pointing the way for our journey to begin.

Chapter 14

———❦———

A sad salute

Ominous clouds and cold wind greeted us on the morning of February 26, 1998, our departure day. Peter suggested I take Scott, Jasper, and Ross for an outing until early afternoon while he dealt with the moving men and the landlord. A nearby mall seemed a good choice for us to while away some time. The boys wandered into a Toys "R" Us store, and I spent fifteen minutes explaining why we couldn't buy any more toys—or anything else for that matter—since our camper was already overflowing.

We ate French fries at a snack bar in the mall as a parade of people strolled by. A little Dutch girl about three years old reminded me of Sierra, and suddenly I felt angry at the girl's mother and wanted to shout, How come you have your little girl, but I don't have mine? As other Dutch people passed by, I felt angry at them, too. Why are you so satisfied here when we weren't? Of course, for all I knew, they could have been unhappy with their lives, too, and stuck in this little corner of the world, unable to alter their course.

Peter and I, on the other hand, were leaping toward a new future. For the second time in a year, we were changing direction. It seemed we were perennially lost, like little rabbits in the woods, and in order to find the right way out, we had to keep hopping around and hoping we weren't going deeper into the forest.

"Can we go now?" Scott asked, breaking into my thoughts. He and his brothers were getting restless. Since it was close to two, we headed back to the Cave to see if it was time to leave.

The moving truck sat in front of the townhouse, and Peter was still helping load in our furniture and boxes. "Maybe you should go to the playground," he said, so I put the kids back in the car and drove to the next village.

On this cold winter afternoon, the playground seemed empty and forlorn, its bright red and blue equipment in stark contrast to the bleak sky. We played on the swings and monkeybars until the boys' cheeks turned rosy and they complained about the cold. I snapped a few photos before we left, commemorating this strange, sad day.

Back at the house, Peter said he was hungry, so the boys and I walked across the street for the last time to buy a take-out dinner at the neighborhood snack bar. We gathered for an impromptu picnic in the living room among the boxes and dust bunnies, feeling invisible as the moving men walked by, carrying our precious things away. Bye, goose girl and your little white goose, I said to myself. See you again some day.

Finally the movers left. Peter and I swept and mopped the floors one last time. The landlord came, inspected the property, gave us back our deposit, and wished us a pleasant journey. We walked out of the Cave and didn't look back.

Dusk was falling, and on the western horizon, glittering sunlight peeked out from a thick blanket of dark gray clouds, a hopeful sign on this otherwise dreary day. The boys and I climbed into the Suburban as Peter hooked up the camper. Then he got in, drove up the hill to turn around, then back down the street, where we passed by our townhouse one last time. On the sidewalk were two neighbors Peter befriended. They stepped out of the warmth of their homes to stand in what seemed a sad salute. We waved and drove on.

—◦◊◦—

After traveling five hours to Trier, Germany, we discovered the campground we had stayed in last fall was closed for the season. Luckily, a nearby McDonald's had a large, well-lit parking area, where we spent a fitful night, trying to sleep while kids in mopeds zoomed around the parking lot.

The next day, as we drove southward, excitement and fear tumbled around inside me. Peter and I had done wild things in the past, but taking off with only a vague itinerary on a six-month trip through Europe was the wildest. As the highway unfurled before us, I wondered whether we'd look back on this adventure as a folly or a necessary step toward the future.

If only we had a firm idea of where to go when this trip was over. On one hand, returning to Virginia Beach made good sense; our house still hadn't sold, and being in a familiar place after all of the anxiety we'd experienced seemed like a good plan, like returning to a safe anchorage. On the other hand, we left Virginia Beach because we felt we needed a change.

Then there were the ghosts. If we returned to our old home, I'd have to face the memories, those images that I could hardly bear to replay in my mind. The hardest image of all was seeing me before Sierra died, a woman so different than I was today. Sometimes it seemed that's what I was running from: the realization that the former me was gone forever. She died when Sierra did. And maybe I still wasn't ready to let go of either one.

The decisions Peter and I made—to move to Europe and then to take this extended camping trip—seemed almost like devices to keep us preoccupied, so caught up in details that we were too busy to stop and think about who we'd become and how Sierra's death had changed us. We didn't want to accept who we were now. We were still stuck in that last picture frame, the one Sierra skipped through, her golden hair shining. Saying farewell to our old selves and embracing new identities felt like putting Sierra into a drawer somewhere, the ultimate betrayal.

After a quick stop to see an old friend in Zurich, where we celebrated Peter's and Scott's birthdays, the highway took us deep into the snowy Swiss Alps. When we emerged south of the St. Gotthard tunnel in Italy, a pink sky glowed, mirrored in the still deep lakes that divide the landscape of Italy's northern region.

"It's the color of summer," I announced, glad finally to have left winter behind.

We planned to stay a week or so in between Verona and Venice and chose a campground near Padua, where we set up camp beside a budding willow tree, its green boughs not only promising spring but also reminding me of the willow tree we planted for Sierra in our yard in Virginia Beach. It felt like a good omen, a greeting from her as our journey began.

That afternoon Peter took Ross for a bike ride through the flat Italian countryside, and I gave Scott and Jasper their first home-schooling lesson. We would concentrate on two subjects each session; today was history and literature. With the setting for Romeo and Juliet so close by, we read a synopsis of Shakespeare's play from our textbook.

"You mean they both die?" Scott said, his eyes wet with tears.

"Yes," I answered. "And all because those two families couldn't learn to get along with each other. But at the very end, they decide to be friends so that their children's deaths won't be in vain. Do you know what that means?"

Scott thought a moment and said, "Does it mean they died for a reason, instead of for no reason?"

"That's right," I said. "Good." Jasper was beginning to squirm a little, so I launched into a lesson about the Roman Empire since we planned to visit a Roman amphitheater in Verona the next day.

But later I wondered about what Scott had said.

Spring surprised us with a snowstorm while we were camped in San Marino, a tiny republic midway down Italy's east coast. Several inches of snow fell in the night, threatening to collapse our voortent, and Peter had to get out of bed to brush the snow off. I snuggled under my sleeping bag, thankful for the warmth of the nearby heater.

The boys slept in the front of the camper in what normally would have been the master bedroom, but Peter removed the bed and fashioned three cots there, one on each wall. We slept in the rear in a bed that converted from the dining room table. It was actually quite comfortable, and for privacy, we simply closed the boys' door. The only down side was having to convert the bed back to a table every morning and then reverse the procedure each night.

As soon as the snow melted, we planned to leave Italy for Greece, a country none of us had ever visited. I once had a friend, Laurie, who came from a Greek family. On Sundays they'd gather at her grandmother's Greek restaurant, Sherrill's, in Washington, D.C., and sometimes I was invited to join them. I remember listening to Laurie's relatives speak Greek, an evocative language that sounded ancient and wise.

Later I became friends with a handsome young Greek named Paul, who gave me a photo of him taken in Greece, standing in front of green rolling hills and a broad sky, tinged in pink. In college I studied Greek drama, mythology, and the gods of Mount Olympus. Soon I would see the fertile breeding ground of western literature, the places where Greek warriors fought their battles and nursed their wounds. Somehow Greece with its tragic tales seemed a fitting place to find solace for my family, shadowed by our own tragic history.

But first we had to leave Italy behind. Peter devised a procedure for breaking camp, a system that had already become automatic. First, he unhooked the power and rolled up the cords. Scott and Jasper helped him fold up the chairs and tables in the voortent. Inside with Ross, I stowed the stuff we'd unpacked a few days before:

the dishes, food, books, toys, coffeemaker, fan, shoes, clothes, and ever-present damp towels.

I stashed the laptop under the seat of the table, anchored the TV with a stretch cord, and stretched another cord across the refrigerator door. This last step was a new one. En route to San Marino after the Suburban had rounded a particularly sharp curve, the refrigerator door flew open, unbeknownst to us, and later we found orange juice, broken glass, yogurt, and leftover chicken spread from one end of the camper to the other—not a pretty sight when you're tired after a long day's journey and just want to fall into bed.

After stowing everything, I took Ross outside for a walk while Peter, Scott, and Jasper loaded in the tables, chairs, carpet, trash can, grill, laundry basket, outdoor lights, and at least a dozen other bulky items essential for a comfortable life on the road. When these were stored in the camper, filling up every inch of available floor space, Peter took down the voortent, folded it up, put it in the camper, and closed the door with a bang—our signal that it was time to go.

Driving south along the Adriatic, I decided the east coast of Italy looked like the Garden of Eden. Lush forests covered hillsides that descended to the sea, and newly plowed fields spread out like quilts at a giant's picnic. I wished we could stop and explore this region, and while we could have if we really wanted, Greece called out to us.

That night we tried to sleep in a rest area behind a gas station as traffic on the adjacent toll road rumbled by nonstop. Suddenly we heard voices outside our camper. Peter lifted the shade, peeked out, and said, "There are three or four guys coming through a hole in the fence. They're up to something."

"What?" I said. The kids were sleeping, but now I was wide awake.

"Shhh," Peter said.

"Do you have your phone?" I whispered.

"No, it's in the car."

"Go get it."

Peter pulled on his pants and casually went out into the night. I lifted the shade cautiously to try to see what was going on. One of the men spoke to Peter, and I held my breath and tried to hear. But Peter came back inside, locked the door, and showed me the phone in his hand. I was pretty sure we didn't know what number to call if we needed help.

"What did they say?"

"All I could make out was bambino. I think they said I should go back in the camper and make a baby." That wasn't very likely to happen—not with these guys milling about.

Soon we saw what they were up to: two of them began unloading contraband—we couldn't see what it was—from a truck parked beside us, and then they handed it bucket-brigade style to two others, who passed it through a hole in the fence, presumably to their mates loading the goods onto a truck on the other side. The men smoked and talked and acted as though this were a normal thing to do at eleven p.m. in the parking lot of a service station by one of Italy's main highways.

"Why are they so casual?" I asked. "They don't even act like they're worried the guy in the truck will wake up."

"They're not worried," Peter answered. "The driver of the truck knows what's going on. He's probably getting a cut of the profits."

We watched until they finished, and I wondered again whether taking this trip was putting my family in unnecessary danger. Peter, who traveled a lot in his younger days, seemed confident that there was nothing to fear in the countries we would visit, most of which he'd been to before. We did take the precaution, however, of removing our U.S. license plates and replacing them with long, narrow European-style plates bearing the same number. "Just to be on the safe side," Peter said.

In fact, of all the countries we would visit, Greece had endured the most terrorist attacks in recent years. And after this strange encounter in the Italian night, I wasn't feeling quite as happy-go-lucky as before. The next day we waited in the dirty, busy port of Brindisi until evening when we could finally pull our camper aboard the ferry and cross the dark waters of the Adriatic east toward the land of the gods.

Chapter 15

—⦿—

Lasting ripples

By the time we arrived in Igoumenitsa the next morning, Peter and I were bleary-eyed after an uncomfortable night on the ferry. For two nights, neither of us had slept well, and now we found ourselves in Greece without a clue where we were going. The kids announced they were hungry, we needed groceries, and the currency exchange place was closed. I just wanted to go home, but we didn't have a home. We were here in this strange country, where I couldn't even read the street signs. I felt so lost. This adventurous existence, barely a few weeks old, suddenly felt like a mistake.

As Peter drove south toward the Peloponnese, where we'd look for a campground, I shared some of my fears. "Where will we end up, Peter? What are we accomplishing by taking this long camping trip and spending all of our money? Shouldn't we be busy settling down somewhere and living a normal life?"

"Slow down, Peggy," Peter said. He pulled off the road and looked at me, his blue eyes red around the edges from lack of sleep. "If you're saying you want to give up on this trip, that's fine. We'll turn around right here right now and get back on that ferry." I glanced at the kids, who were listening and wondering where this discussion would lead. Even Ross, who was too young to understand, seemed to sense this was a turning point and sucked even more vigorously on his thumb.

"I don't know, Peter. I'm just scared. After the last couple of days, I'm not sure if we should be dragging our kids on this crazy trip. It feels like we're going in circles."

"The kids are fine, Peggy," Peter said. "Don't worry about them. Think how lucky they are to spend so much time with us. You know kids want that more than anything. And that's not even counting the history and art and culture they'll learn. And even if they don't have many memories of this trip when they're older, it will influence them for the rest of their lives."

When I didn't say anything, Peter continued, "You're the one I'm worried about. You need to relax and enjoy this trip, Peg. Think how lucky you are to have a six-month vacation in Europe with your family. Who cares if we spend all of our money? We can always make more. Just don't let this trip be ruined by 'what if's' and second thoughts. We're in Greece now. Look around. It's beautiful here. We'll find a nice campground, and everything will be fine. I promise."

Peter smiled at me, and I smiled back, knowing he was right. I needed to find pleasure in the moment, relish the simple joys of being with my husband and children as we shared a trip of a lifetime. This was an incredible chance to renew our spirits and grow closer as a family. I thought about how easy it was to talk to Peter and how thankful I felt that we'd learned to air our feelings and not let them fester inside. When we first lived together, I didn't know how to express my feelings very well, but Peter taught me how.

Now riding beside Peter many years later, our three sons in the back seat, as we continued our amazing journey, I reflected on the road before us and the one behind. I considered our little girl, who had bounded through our lives for a brief splash of time, yet left behind lasting ripples. Sometimes it almost seemed as if Peter and I were asleep while she was here. When we woke up, she was gone.

—◦◦◦—

A lovely campground in Ancient Olympia opened the same day we arrived, and we had the whole place to ourselves. Perched atop a hill, the campground overlooked snow-capped mountains to the north. We spread out on two campsites under mimosa trees and set up house for a week. So far we'd taken our time traveling through Europe, which is just what Peter and I wanted to do.

As travelers, we can be greedy sometimes, devouring cities and countries as if we're at a sumptuous banquet, but don't really have time to savor the dishes. At the end of the meal, we try to recall what we've swallowed as the tastes and textures swirl around in a forgotten stew. Isn't it better to savor a simple meal whose distinctive flavors linger on your tongue?

Food was high on our list of priorities on this trip: shopping, preparing meals, and eating took up a lot of our energy. I became somewhat obsessed by grocery stores in the foreign countries we visited. Each one was a cultural treasure chest. Sometimes Peter just dropped me off, saying he'd be back in an hour. He knew how long it would take me to decipher labels, to figure out how many drachmas equaled how many dollars, to decide if a bottle of wine was sweet or dry. Yet in the process, I was becoming Greek—at least for a little while. Beside me the local folks did their daily shopping, and I tried to blend in, to not be a tourist, to adopt a different identity.

Perhaps traveling through so many countries would be my way of finding a new identity. As I tried on different personas, I wanted to shed the pieces of me that needed to be let go. While I hoped this trip would help me grow stronger, more at peace, at the same time I didn't want to leave Sierra behind, like a cast-off piece of clothing that didn't fit anymore. How could I keep her as a part of me, yet lose the sadness her death had brought to my life?

The first Olympic Games were held here in Ancient Olympia, and we explored the remnants of the old city on a lovely spring morning in late March. Strolling amid the ruins of temples and columns, Peter and I talked to the boys about epic heroes, the Greek gods, and mythical creatures.

"How did the temples fall down?" Scott asked.

"Christians came along in the third and fourth centuries and knocked them over," I answered.

"Why?"

"Because they didn't want people to worship false gods."

Scott thought a moment. "What's a false god?"

"A different one," I said and found it hard to elaborate. Peter and I had strayed from religion in the years since Sierra died. I continued to believe in God, to be certain heaven existed and Sierra was waiting there for me, but a sense of anger still simmered inside, anger at God for knocking down my perfect life and strewing it in pieces, just as the columns of these temples lay haphazardly on the ground.

Down deep, a different kind of anger ate away like poison at my insides. I was angry at the world, at Peter, at myself. I was even angry at Sierra. I needed to learn how to forgive.

—◦◦◦—

That night Peter and I arranged for a babysitter to come to the camper, so we could go out. It was our first time away from the kids in the month since we started our journey, and we found a tree-lined terrace, ordered an apértif, and savored some grown-up time.

"So what do you think of this traveling life?" Peter asked.

"I could keep doing this forever," I answered with a smile.

We sat in silence and listened to men at a nearby table, speaking their native tongue. As the day darkened, birds flew overhead finishing their daily tasks, finding one last morsel of food for their hatchlings. My mind wandered to our sons, probably getting ready for bed in the camper, and suddenly I ached for them. Spending twenty-four hours a day with my family was a strange phenomenon. Normally something of a loner, I was discovering I loved being with my kids so much. We were all getting along well, and I knew it was a gift to be on this adventure with them.

"Where do you think we'll end up?" Peter asked.

"I don't know. Virginia Beach is an easy choice because we know our way around there. Plus the kids would love to go back. And our house is still waiting for us." We had a buyer, but he reneged after renting it for a while. Now we were once again sending mortgage payments to the U.S.

"But after the trip, we can go anywhere," Peter said. "We'll sell the house. I'll fix it up while you and the kids start out someplace new."

I shook my head. "We just did that, Peter, and I don't think I can handle it again. We've made so many bad choices lately."

"We still have time to think about it," Peter said.

Inside I was wondering how long I could keep going with this big question mark looming. I needed a plan, and Virginia Beach was looking more like it. Maybe we needed to go back, to go full circle, to close the loop, to don our new identities in the same place where our old ones ended. Maybe this whole attempt to leave was meant to bring us back to the place it all started, to be able to come face to face with what happened, and to be able to say, "It's O.K. Sierra died, but we didn't." We only had to assimilate her life into ours, to weave our lives together instead of pushing Sierra and her memories away.

A crowded restaurant with spicy smells lured us in, and we ate a tasty dinner of lamb kebabs, olives, and Greek salad. Later we strolled along the main street and dropped by a souvenir shop to look around. The owner, who introduced herself in excellent English, told us she used to live in Canada as a little girl. Dora chatted amiably with us about President Clinton's indiscretions, currently making headlines, and the upcoming Greek Orthodox Easter that promised to be a cultural treat.

"You remind me of someone I know," Dora said to me suddenly. "It's a sad story...." and she drifted off.

"What happened?" Peter asked.

"About four months ago, a terrible accident happened here in Olympia. The train hit a car, and two children were killed and one boy was hurt very bad. He's in the States now trying to get better. His mom's there with him. Jenny. She's American. That's who you remind me of." Dora paused, then added, "Jenny's daughter was one of the two children killed."

"Who was driving?" I asked, horrified by the news of this local tragedy.

"Jenny's husband."

"How awful," I said, shaking my head. Then Peter and I told Dora that we too had lost a child and shared Sierra's story. When we were finished, Dora told us her father had drowned in Canada when she was a little girl, watching from the shore. After that her mother decided to move to Greece, to be with family, bringing her young children with her.

As we stood in this brightly lit gift shop cluttered with t-shirts and trinkets, the world seemed small—as if the sadness of the planet linked us together. One thing I'd learned during the aftermath of Sierra's death was how much sadness the world holds. Now I thought about Jenny in the U.S. with her son, whose injuries were so severe he might never recover. I thought about Jenny's husband, who crossed the tracks at the wrong moment, shattering his world. I pictured Dora as a little girl, watching from the shore as her father drowned. And I felt very sad.

Dora said she wished I could speak Greek because the mother of the other child who died wasn't doing very well.

"It will take a long time before she feels better," I said.

The next day I heard the train's whistle, and I remembered Jenny and her son and the others whose lives were irrevocably altered four months ago. So many people faced tragedies every day, their lives shattered into small shards, like a broken mirror that can never be pieced back together.

Chapter 16

———∽∿∽———

Treasuring memories

After circling around the bottom of the Peloponnese, we landed in Corinth at a seaside campground that looked and felt like heaven. I could easily see why the gods chose Greece as their home: it's idyllic. At Isthmius Beach Camping, orange and lemon trees surrounded our camper. The sidewalk to the bathhouse was lined with waist-high geraniums, fire bursts of color against velvety green leaves. Above us yellow-gold blooms of prickly pear decorated the hillsides.

But it was the oranges and lemons that spilled from the trees and scented the air with sweet perfume that tempted my senses. When I asked at the office if I could pick a few pieces of fruit, the woman said, "No," and then laughed. "You must pick many fruits." And we did. We drank pulpy, fresh-squeezed orange juice for breakfast and tart-sweet lemonade throughout the day.

Homeschooling was going well. I decided to give Scott and Jasper mid-term exams and devised study guides about Shakespeare and Greek mythology. We practiced math problems and studied science. To everyone's delight, both boys made B's on their exams, and I congratulated myself for keeping their minds busy.

Part of our schoolwork involved keeping journals. I wrote mine on a laptop and sent electronic dispatches back to family and friends in the U.S, who were following our journey. The boys used old-fashioned tools—pen and paper—to write in theirs. Since Scott and Jasper weren't particularly fond of writing, I created fill-in-the-blank journal pages. They drew a picture of something they'd seen, noted the date, place, and weather. Then they wrote the "best thing we did today," "something I learned today," and "something I want to learn more about." At the bottom they added a sentence or two about a "funny/special/scary thing that happened today." The boys complained about writing in their journals, but I knew one day they'd treasure these memories.

After Sierra died, I wrote in my journal with a vengeance. My heart bled on those pages. Now reading those journal entries brought me a mixture of pain and joy because mixed in with the sadness, anger, fear, disbelief, guilt, and hopelessness, I wrote down my memories of Sierra—her favorite foods, cute sayings, little habits. When I first recorded these small details, I believed I could never possibly forget them, but in fact memories of Sierra grew dimmer with each passing year. I was afraid of losing her.

She used to say, "Are you proud of me, Mommy?" when she'd do something to please me. She often held pieces of candy tightly in her fist until they melted or turned to mush. She lined up her raisins on her placemat in neat lines. One of her favorite sayings was, "It's a good great day,"

I used to say to Sierra, "Are you my happy girl?"

It seems we never recognize the happiest moments of our lives until, looking back, we see them and know.

———

In Athens we bought shoes for the boys, and the woman at the shop said in her broken English that Scott looked like Christ and kissed him on both cheeks. She gave the children candy, and we smiled and said thank you, feeling strangely bothered by her display of affection.

At the Tomb of the Unknown Soldier, as we watched the changing of the guards ceremony—tassel-topped men marching with strange shuffle steps and serious countenances, a drunk guy made a scene, and the police arrived with flashing lights and sirens and took him away. Peter and I laughed, but inside I worried about terrorists and didn't feel comfortable in this busy city.

The Acropolis swarmed with tourists, just the prompting we needed to leave Athens for more peaceful surroundings. Tranquility awaited in Delphi, where a picturesque campground overlooking acres of olive trees became our temporary home. It was Greek Easter weekend, and Scott and Jasper were delighted to see kids at the campground. They immediately befriended Lambros, a handsome boy who spoke a little English, and together they played with Lambros' remote-controlled car, sending it careening across the marble floors of the bathhouse.

We visited the Oracle of Delphi in a stunning mountain setting, and I recalled the role this Oracle played in shaping the events of the Ancient Greeks. I wished I could approach this venerated being and learn what our future held.

That night a sitter watched the boys, and Peter and I went to Easter Mass in Itea, a nearby town. I'd never been to a Greek Orthodox service and found it fascinating to watch the people—young and old alike—kiss an icon of the Virgin Mary upon entering the church. The priests stood in front and recited scripture, but no one seemed to listen. Crowds came and went until a candle-lighting ceremony began. From one candle everyone lit candles, and we all went out into the street, shielding our candle flames from the wind. Then everyone began to sing. It was a beautiful sight, and I thought of Sierra and imagined I saw her face in the dancing flames. She seemed close by, and I shivered in the cool night air. At midnight fireworks exploded overhead, and Peter and I agreed this was a spectacular way to celebrate Jesus' rising from the dead.

Back at the campground we dined in the restaurant, a late night tradition, on luscious lamb slices and soup made of lamb's blood. As Peter and I ate, I thought about Jesus' death and resurrection, about Sierra and her life, and wondered if my own rebirth were near.

Back in Italy, we drove west toward Pompeii, a place that had captured my imagination since I was young. At a campground close to the ancient city, we met a Danish family, the Landers, en route to Greece for a month's holiday. My kids happily played with their children, and Peter and I invited Annette and her husband, Peter, over for dinner.

"What did you like best about Greece?" Annette asked.

"The people," Peter said. "They were so friendly and helpful." We told them a few stories about being lost and kind folks who helped us find our way.

"What did you like, Peggy?"

"It's cheap there!" Everyone laughed. "No, I liked the beaches on the western coast of the Peloponnese—just gorgeous and totally undeveloped."

The conversation turned to our meeting with Dora in Ancient Olympia and then of course to Sierra.

"I think we're still trying to run away from our sadness," I said to Annette as I refilled our wine glasses. "But I don't think we can. It would be better to stop running and let the ghosts catch up with us. Maybe it's time to let Sierra's death become a part of our lives."

"Do you think you can stop running?" Peter Landers asked.

"I think we'll get tired of it sooner or later. It takes a lot of energy to run away from something. But I think we need to find the right time to face our ghosts."

"But who are they?" Annette asked. "It's not Sierra you're running from, is it?"

"No," I answered and took a swallow of wine. "I think it's us."

Pompeii was full of ghosts, and as we walked with the children through the city the next day, I felt as if I were trespassing on hallowed land. Two thousand people perished the day Mt. Vesuvius erupted, and a permanent silent scream seemed to echo among the crumbling walls.

Scattered throughout the city were plaster casts of bodies placed in the exact positions in which they had been found. We saw a child in the embrace of a mother. Somewhere else a dog lay next to his master. Pompeii seemed spooky and sad and strange all at the same time, a reminder of how small and helpless we are.

Suddenly I realized these Pompeiians died of asphyxiation, the same thing that Sierra died of. I couldn't wait to leave this doomed city, which represented a tragic chapter of the world's past, one of many times when nature reared its ugly head and thousands perished.

After a few days in Rome and Florence, I was ready to leave Italy. May had arrived, and we hadn't even been to France or Spain. Money was going fast, especially with our gas-guzzling Suburban, campsites fees, gas, food, and incidentals, which in total averaged $500 per week, not including the mortgage payment we were sending to the U.S., car and health insurance, and storage fees.

Would we have enough to get home? I wondered and then remembered I didn't even know where home was anymore.

The South of France was the one place Peter and I had talked about moving to before we settled on Maastricht. After setting up camp in a lush campground in Antibes, we sat in the shade of a tall evergreen, enjoying the warm, gentle breezes blowing from the coast about a mile away. The kids played nearby while Peter and I sipped glasses of wine. "To think that we could have moved here instead of cold, drizzly Holland," he said.

"O.K., you were right, Peter. It is nicer here."

"We can still move to France," he said with a gleam in his eye.

"You can. I'm heading back to Virginia Beach," I said, only half kidding.

"Are you sure, Peg?"

"Yep, I'm sure. I need to know where we're going, and it seems crazy to try to start a new dream in a new place after what happened in Maastricht."

"Has it been a total failure, Peggy?"

"No, definitely not. This trip has been incredible. Traveling was one of the reasons I wanted to move to Europe in the first place. I just didn't think it would happen all at once."

"I only hope you don't think we've wasted our time. You often focus on the negative, Peg. You should look around you."

How could I not notice the good things around me? I wondered, watching Scott and Jasper ride their bikes happily in the lane and Ross fiddle with his toys in the grass. Across from me Peter sat in a canvas folding chair, relaxed and handsome with his salt-and-pepper beard, straw hat, and a denim shirt that brought out the blue in his eyes.

Travel agreed with me, too. I was becoming thinner, tanned, more physically fit. Somehow I had to learn to let go of my fears and worries and appreciate the moment of time I'm in. Maybe that was the lesson I needed to learn on this journey: to appreciate the wealth of good in my life instead of worrying about the things I can't control.

Traveling in this random way, not sure where we would be from day to day, was good practice for me. When Sierra died, I felt such a loss of control over my life. Her death was a cosmic slap in the face, maybe even God's way of reminding me that I wasn't really in charge. Yet would a kind, loving God seek to teach me a lesson in such a tragic way? It made no sense to think that was the reason she died.

I was beginning to learn one lesson at least: to stop worrying about perfection, to accept that there will always be things that we can't change.

Chapter 17

—◦◦◦—

Exactly this moment

Leah, an 18-year-old from California, bounced into our lives in Antibes. Recommended by the campground office, she came to babysit one night so Peter and I could go on a rare date. Bubbly and vivacious, Leah said she'd been traveling in Europe for a couple of months but was worried she'd have to head home early since she was low on money.

"We've been looking for an au pair to travel with us and help with the kids," I said spontaneously. Peter looked at me as if I'd lost my mind. We just met Leah after all.

"It's just a thought. We can talk about it later," I said and gave Leah instructions for the boys' dinner and bedtimes.

That evening Peter and I explored Cannes, which was busy preparing for its annual film festival. Workmen built stages, laid red carpets, and put up posters of the festival's film schedule. The city reeled with passion.

On a side street a fashionable café full of well-dressed young people enticed us. Sitting down at the bar, we drank anise-flavored Pernod on the rocks, served with a spicy olive tapenade and toasted bread. Jazz played in the background, and Peter and I relaxed among the colorful crowd, content to sit and simply enjoy a break from the kids. Later we ate beef brochettes on an outdoor terrace and watched the stars slowly pop out of the night sky. I thought of F. Scott and Zelda Fitzgerald and how—not far from here—their turbulent lives brought them from ecstasy to despair. Even in a place as magical as the South of France, happiness is never guaranteed.

After discussing it further, Peter and I invited Leah to join us for a month as the boys' au pair. She would travel with us through Spain and Portugal, and we'd make sure she got back to Nice in time to catch her flight to California. The boys liked Leah. We all did. She smiled a lot, took care of herself, and had a calm way about her. And while the five of us had relished our time together, it was wonderful to have a new person to talk to.

After exploring Provence, following the footsteps of van Gogh in Arles, and biking through the countryside in Avignon, we traveled to Barcelona, a city I had mixed feelings about. One summer while backpacking, I visited Barcelona and found it a little seedy. That's probably because my girlfriend and I were accosted in the Plaza Real by a couple of Spaniards, who became offended that we didn't want to join them. They hurled obscenities at us, and we scurried off, no harm done. But the experience left me wary of Spain in general and Barcelona in particular.

For good reason, it turned out. At the campground one evening, Peter and the boys washed dishes in the sink at the bathhouse while Leah and I cleaned up after dinner at our campsite. A guy on the other side of a chain-link fence in a security uniform called me over. As I walked toward him, he pointed downward, and I saw he was exposing himself. Leah came up behind me. "Let's go inside," I said quietly. She saw why and let out a small shriek as we sought safety in the camper. Even though we knew that the weirdo couldn't reach us through the chain-link fence, we were frightened. When Peter came back, I told him I wanted to leave this campground and Barcelona as soon as we could. It still was not my favorite place.

Spain's southern shores were more to my liking. We wound up in Benidorm, a busy tourist town on Spain's southeast coast, full of Dutch and German tourists. I could easily see why they were here. Spain was cheap, and the weather practically ideal: perfect for lounging on the beach and exploring hill towns. One evening, thanks to Leah, Peter and I went out for paella.

As the sun sank into the sea, Peter and I found a restaurant that bordered a walking street. Soon the Spanish townspeople appeared, parading in their best clothes. I saw one man, a Spanish version of Tom Wolfe, wearing white from head to toe: white suit, shirt, vest, tie, socks, shoes, and, of course, a white hat. Parents escorted daughters, whose beaux loped along under the watchful eyes of Papa. I thought of Sierra when I saw the pretty girls, and instead of feeling sorry for myself, I tried something new. I thought of a happy memory instead.

Peter and I managed to take only one real vacation when Sierra was alive. In 1989, a year before she died, we drove to Canada and Vermont. Pregnant with Jasper, I found the trip overwhelming at times, but also rich in wonder. Traveling with children opens your eyes to new sights and smells, reminding you to stop and notice the small joys just under your nose, the ones you rarely see—unless a child grabs your arm and says, "Look!" and points to a bee gathering nectar from a flower shaped like a bell.

My memories of that vacation are full of such look-and-see moments. We stayed a few days with my dad and his wife, Marilyn, at their summer house in the Thousand Islands, where we swam in the St. Lawrence, boated through narrow channels, and swung happily in a hammock under birch trees, dappled by sunlight that filtered through the leaves.

From Ontario, the four of us headed east across New York to Burlington, Vermont, a city that charmed me with its down-home atmosphere. One morning we ate breakfast in an old-timey coffee shop with Formica tabletops and vinyl booths. Locals greeted each other with "Howdy-do's," steaming mugs in hand. I savored the scent of maple syrup mingling with the smell of fried bacon and fresh-brewed coffee. Scott and Sierra loved their pancakes and hot chocolate, and Peter and I felt rich with boundless blessings.

After breakfast, a nearby museum offered a few hours of entertainment: trains, large and small, an antique toy collection, big barns, old tools, and room to run around. On a blanket spread in the grass, the four of us ate sandwiches and chips. Then while the children napped in the back seat, Peter and I motored through rolling hills, past farmhouses with weathervanes and piles of neatly stacked wood. I remember saying, "Let's move to Vermont," and Peter's response: "Brrrrr. Too cold."

The next day we ate ice cream at Ben and Jerry's and explored a wildflower farm, where buzzing insects filled the air. We took photos of Scott and Sierra in front of a field ablaze with color. That day has stayed so clear in my mind, as if it were yesterday. I still smell the meadow and feel the warm sun. I see Sierra in her hand-me-down wool sweater and faded denim overalls, her yellow hair like a halo around her face. Back then I would never have guessed those moments with her would be so precious and few, to be played in my mind over and over again like a favorite film.

Snapping back to the present, I watched Benidorm's colorful street scene play out in front of me. Even here, even now, Sierra offered a lesson to me, a simple one, really, not new. In fact, I already knew it. But if I thought of this lesson as a gift from Sierra, maybe it would mean more, and in the days ahead, I would hold it in my hand, like a melting piece of candy, while searching for that abstract place called home.

The lesson was this: we only have exactly this moment, the one we're in. We only have the people around us for this rare piece of time. The light only shines through the trees, dappling our faces with light and dark dots, for just this fraction of a second. We can only hear the music of a child's laughter during these few minutes that we have right now. This life we're given has no guarantee, no promise of tomorrow—which means the gifts we have precisely at this juncture of time and space may be the best gifts we'll ever have.

"I love you, Peter," I said as the candle flame on our table fluttered in the evening breeze. He grabbed my hand and smiled. I think he sensed I was figuring something out, something that would help us reach home.

———✸———

In Portugal's Algarve region, we found a picturesque campground, dotted with gnarly olive trees, like wizened ancestors from another age. Atop our hilly campsite, only a mile inland, we could glimpse the Atlantic. It was pure paradise.

When Peter was in his mid-twenties, he lived in Lagos, Portugal, not far from where we were staying. He and his family escaped the cold climate of the Netherlands to live in Lagos for two years, where they ran a snack bar in the center of town. Even back then Peter felt unhappy in his birth country and left its confining borders for new horizons. When Peter's mom developed health problems, however, they had to return to the Netherlands. That was twenty years ago, and now Peter was anxious to see what had become of his snack bar and how Lagos had changed.

The first place we visited was the home Peter and his family rented on a hillside overlooking town. Since it appeared uninhabited, we got out of the car and looked around. Peter seemed distracted as we walked on the rocky soil. He was wandering back through the years, back to another time when he and his family lived an idyllic life in the Portuguese countryside.

"That was my room over there," he said, pointing to a window on the left side of the house.

"What an incredible view," I commented as I turned to face the coast below.

"You should see the sunsets from up here."

Peter looked over his shoulder one last time as we drove away, and I knew he was thinking about his long-ago life and where it had led him.

—◦◦◦—

Lagos had changed completely in the twenty years since Peter left. He could barely find his former business. Weaving through narrow streets in the town center, we finally located it: a pizza restaurant now, bearing little resemblance to the old snack bar where Peter and his family sold the "best hamburgers in town." Peter looked sad as he walked around this busy city, no longer the sleepy town he had once known and loved.

In the farmers' market, Peter bumped into his butcher from the old days and remembered enough Portuguese to have a brief chat. He felt better now—as if those years in Lagos were somehow validated. Seeing his butcher made that part of his life real, not just some faraway dream that perhaps never happened at all.

For isn't that what our past often seems? A dream, a separate entity, not real? Sometimes it's as though the past never happened. I felt that way when I thought of Sierra, as if she were just a dream, as if the time she lived on this earth with me and Peter and Scott and Jasper was a fantasy, a vision, shimmering in gold light.

What was in front of me now—Peter, walking beside me, smiling again; Scott and Jasper, sunburned, eating ice cream cones; and Leah, who'd become a friend and confidant, pushing Ross in the stroller—we were what was real. Sierra, who lived, breathed, and brightened my life, was gone, living only in the memory of those who loved her.

I thought about the beauty of a rainbow after a storm and how its soft pastel colors transform a turbulent sky into a vision of hope. Sierra was my rainbow now, real, but distant, and I was finally learning to appreciate her from afar.

Chapter 18

—⟶⟵—

Connected to the past

Up Portugal's coast we drove, past forests and castles and craggy cliffs. With each passing kilometer, I appreciated Portugal more. Like Greece, it resonated with history and, in places, still seemed stuck a few centuries back. Maybe that was why these rustic countries appealed so much to me: they remained connected to their past as I was to mine.

At our campground near Lisbon, Ross made friends with our neighbors, whose campsite was strewn with children's toys. "For our grandchildren when they come to visit," the woman said. She asked us where we were from and said she wanted to share a special treat with us. Later that afternoon, her husband carried over a pot of snails floating in garlicky broth and offered it to us with a smile.

"Obrigado," we said and promised to bring the pot back when we were done. Inside were a hundred tiny snails, each no bigger than a nickel, the kind you see inching up tall reeds, their funny little antenna probing their surroundings. Peter said it had probably taken the family an hour at least to collect all the snails they cooked for us.

At dinner, we ate the snails. Using toothpicks, we poked into the shell, pulling out tiny pieces of meat. Everyone, even the kids, dutifully sampled one. When I tasted mine, it reminded me of a clam—slightly chewy, very salty, and redolent of garlic. Scott and Jasper grimaced, swallowing their snails with difficulty, and Peter and Leah decided the little critters weren't to their liking. However, I continued to eat the snails, not because I loved the way they tasted, but because I didn't want to insult the neighbors. I wanted to do justice to their kindness, to appreciate the gesture by consuming as many as I could.

Sharing our neighbor's food was a way of connecting with them. Throughout our trip, the people whose paths we crossed had added a richer dimension to our travels. Each one offered a lesson, beginning back in Zurich at the beginning of our trip when we met a stylish couple about our age, dressed in black leather, who'd stopped to admire our camper.

"Gypsies," Peter whispered as they walked away. "This is their favorite kind of camper."

Peter explained that our German-built Weipert was practically synonymous with gypsies. And sure enough, whenever we passed a gypsy camp during our travels, we would spot campers like ours. Every so often, as we barreled down the highways of Europe, convoys of campers like ours—gypsies on the move—passed by, going in the other direction. They almost always waved.

I wondered what it would be like to join a gypsy camp for a while, to see firsthand what it would be like to live on the fringes of society. To some extent, I was jealous of their devil-may-care lifestyle. Peter said gypsies are a close-knit bunch and don't welcome outsiders. Maybe that was why I related to them so much. I felt as if we were outsiders now. We'd left the mainstream and were making our own unique path through the world.

Unlike most gypsies, who preferred to stay just outside of society's boundaries, I knew we'd return to our normal lives once more. However, by living this vagabond life for a while, by becoming gypsies of a sort, we were learning to concentrate on the basics of life, the bonds between us, the love we share, the meaningful conversations, and the moments of discovery and joy. We were learning to live in the present again, instead of always looking over our shoulders for a glimpse of a golden-haired girl.

Nearly everyone we'd met on this journey had somehow informed our search for home. I thought of Dora in Ancient Olympia and her sad tale of the train wreck and the long-reaching ripples that emanated from that family tragedy. Of course, Sierra's death still affected us, too, but you can't compare tragedies. Each one has the potential to derail your life. The challenge becomes— for everyone who suffers a terrible loss—getting back up, dusting yourself off, and carrying on. That's what this trip was about for us: finding our way back to the place we left behind that day in August when Sierra silently disappeared from our lives.

As I considered other people we'd met who enriched us in some way, I thought of Antonio, a kind man Peter met in a park in Athens while I homeschooled the older boys back at the camper. As Ross played, Antonio chatted with Peter and invited us to visit him and his wife in their summer home near Delphi.

A week later on a blustery spring day, Peter, the boys, and I snaked along curving mountain roads and found their cottage, simple and small with a large patio overlooking tall mountains and fields full of wildflowers. Antonio's wife, Angelina, who spoke no English but smiled a lot, served cookies and rich, black coffee, the kind that leaves a layer of fine grounds in the bottom of your cup. Antonio showed us around—first, his beehives, where he collected honey; next, the olive trees, whose harvest he pressed into olive oil the color of sunlight; then, the vineyard, where he grew grapes to make flavorful homemade wine.

Afterwards on our way back to the campground, Peter said, "Antonio is a rich man. He has everything he needs in that small house. It's not fancy, but it's home."

Leaving Portugal behind, we hurried across Spain. Two friends from Virginia would join us in a few days, and we needed to meet them in Bayonne, France, on June 16. This meant skipping Madrid and a few other Spanish cities we wished we had time to explore. But we didn't. Our future was calling us, rattling its cage, reminding us that we had to return to our normal lives. "Hurry back!" it said with a growl. "You've been away too long."

Somewhere in Spain we chanced upon an amazing sight. Under a cloudless sky of deep blue, a sea of sunflowers spread across a plain in every direction. I'd never seen so many sunflowers: giant blooms with heads as big as mine facing westward toward the sun, like worshippers paying homage. The combination of colors—golden centers encircled by yellow petals against a jungle of green leaves—made this a dream of a picture for a photographer, a painter, or anyone who happened by and wanted to remember the magic of a moment in Spain.

"We should stop and take some pictures," Peter said.

I looked in the back at Ross asleep in his car seat and knew he'd surely wake up if we stopped. Besides we had miles to go before arriving at the next campground.

"No," I said. "Let's keep going. I'm sure we'll see more sunflowers down the road." But we never did.

Later as we strolled in the shadowy evening near our campsite in Salamanca, Peter said, "We should have stopped." Above us in the purple sky bats swooped in a joyful dance. Under our feet wild thyme crunched, its pungent, earthy smell hovering around us like a ghost.

"I know," I said. "It's like a lot of things in life. We think things will stay the same. They don't, do they?"

Peter didn't answer. He just walked quietly along.

"Or we think we can go back to the way things were," I said.

"You know what's really sad," Peter said, sounding as if he were in a far-off place, "is when we have everything we need and don't appreciate it."

After spending two rainy days camped in the hills above San Sebastian, a city of taverns and narrow streets crowded with fresh-faced youth, we drove northward across the border into France, where we found a tranquil campground in a small village called Bidart.

Right on time our friends Emily and Missy arrived in Bayonne by train from Paris. Packing tents and camping gear, they were thrilled to be in Europe, each for the first time. Our gang of eight filled the Suburban to overflowing, but we were all in vacation mode now, happy to be with friends, enjoying good weather, and living for the moment in this remarkable corner of the world.

Neither Peter nor I had ever been to the Basque coast of France, and we fell in love with its distinctive charm and friendly people. Situated next to the Bay of Biscay, this region with its sandy beaches, green mountains, Alpine architecture, and unique language traces its roots back to cavemen days. We spent days roaming the countryside and exploring small villages.

One tranquil afternoon we found ourselves at the beginning of the Camino de Santiago high up in the Pyrenees Mountains near the Spanish border. Every year thousands of pilgrims follow the trail across the rooftop of Spain westward to a small church that houses St. James' holy relics. On this remote mountaintop, we found rows and rows of makeshift wooden crosses, most made of two sticks clumsily bound together with twine. Attached to these crosses were the names of the pilgrims and the dates they began their holy walk.

The atmosphere was serene and strange. If you listened to the wind, you could almost hear the whispers of all the pilgrims who had come here—perhaps running from their own ghosts—to begin their journey toward redemption. I wondered if our journey since Sierra died was a pilgrimage of sorts. Perhaps this long road we'd been on ever since that steamy August afternoon in 1990 was part of a mysterious plan. The answer depends on whether you believe we're pawns shuffling across the chessboard of life or kings and queens who invent the world we live in.

Choice, however, implies responsibility, and as I returned in my mind to Sierra's death, I preferred to think the matter was not in my hands or in Peter's. Rather it was an accident, an event that no one could have prevented because it was somehow meant to happen. I still yearned to find a reason for Sierra's death, but the answer remained out there, beyond the sea of sunflowers. Maybe I would find it one day, but for now I contented myself with the brief moments of clarity and solace I found in the places we visited.

The wind blew on the mountaintop, and the June sun beat down. Scott and Jasper ran in circles around the crosses. We posed for photos, climbed into the car, and drove down from the mountain into the valley below.

Chapter 19

———⟨⟨⟨⟩⟩⟩———

A forgotten dream

After a few days in Bidart, France, we journeyed inland toward the Dordogne, a region east of Bordeaux. It was beautiful there, like a forgotten dream. While our campground offered every modern convenience, including a pool, bikes for rent, and kids' activities, the surrounding countryside seemed frozen in time, offering a glimpse into centuries past.

Nearby a small village encircled a huge castle, which for a small fee we explored one afternoon. Having left Scott and Jasper with Leah at the pool, Peter, Emily, Missy, Ross, and I spent an hour or two peeking into dusty rooms and imagining what it would be like to live a nobleman's life. The brochure said the baron who lived here owned the rolling hills and forests from the chateau to the distant horizon.

There was something about the Dordogne that touched my soul: a forlornness. Empty roads carved through still forests and golden meadows, cresting hills and descending into valleys. I took long hikes in the countryside around our campground, sometimes with only my thoughts to keep me company, other times with Peter or Missy or Emily. My college friends were enjoying their visit in Europe, and for the most part, Peter and I were happy to have them. Yet sometimes it seemed their presence distracted me from the work I felt compelled to do: learning to live in the present while sorting out the past and preparing for the future.

One afternoon I told everyone I was taking a hike, and Leah asked if she could come along. She would leave the next day to travel by train south to Nice, where she'd catch her flight to California. In the month that we'd traveled together, Leah and I had grown close, and at times I felt as if she were my daughter, too. Peter and I invited her to visit us in Virginia one day, and I hoped we'd stay in touch.

The trail we chose circled a large pond and crossed over fields leading toward a majestic forest. After a few minutes of walking in silence, we stopped to admire the way the clouds changed colors as the sun dropped in the sky. Suddenly Leah touched my arm and looked at me, her freckled face serious for a change, her green eyes peering deep into mine. "There's something I've been wanting to tell you, Peggy," she said. I waited for her to continue.

"I met Sierra once."

"You what?"

"I met Sierra—well, she came to me in a vision back in California."

"A vision?"

"Yeah, it was weird. This little blonde girl about three years old sort of appeared before me." Leah paused as if trying to find the right words. I stood there speechless, waiting for her to continue.

"Anyway, this little girl came to me, and it was like she wanted to tell me something. I couldn't get her message, though. And after about a minute, she went away."

Leah stopped to gather her thoughts, then began again. "I couldn't figure out who she was, and I kind of forgot about her. When I met you and Peter and you told me about Sierra and showed me pictures of her, I remembered this vision of her."

I stammered, "How do you know it was Sierra?"

"I just do," Leah said. "I'm sure of it. I only wish I knew what she was trying to tell me."

We started walking again and entered the forest, its towering pines forming a roof overhead while at our feet leafy ferns carpeted the forest floor. We walked silently, and I considered Leah's revelation. This wasn't the first time I'd heard that Sierra had come to visit. Peter's sister, Karin, said Sierra pops in every now and then and once even gave Karin a message for us: that she was doing fine and wanted us to be happy.

While I wanted to believe in these visits, they seemed so unreal to me. Maybe I was jealous that Sierra visited others. Besides appearing in an occasional dream, she never communicated with me. What an amazing thing it would be if she did, what a relief to know she was all right. Instead, it seemed I was always destined to be her worried mother, standing at the front door, one hand shading my eyes as I scanned the horizon, forever seeking my little girl.

I knew what Peter would think when I told him about Leah's visit from Sierra. He'd scoff and shake his head, not one to believe in this psychic stuff. But, unlike Peter, I wanted to believe and wondered if this were another example of destiny, of fate. If it were true that Leah had met Sierra, then that meant meeting Leah in Antibes was destined somehow, that all the events that swirled through our lives were part of some master plan. If I could believe that, then I could absolve myself of the responsibility of Sierra's death. I could free myself of the guilt that remained deep in my bones, that I could never seem to shake.

It seemed too easy to say that I wasn't in control, to say we're like leaves being scattered by the wind, every which way, and whatever we choose to do or not to do doesn't influence the ultimate path we follow. I thought about Ross and whether he'd even exist if Sierra hadn't died. I thought about Scott and Jasper and how Sierra's death had affected their lives. I thought about Peter and me and how much we'd changed as a result of Sierra's death.

I might never know whether Sierra's death was meant to be. But I was learning that I couldn't blame Sierra's death for my unhappiness. That would be like saying Sierra herself was to blame because if she had never existed, I would never have gotten so sad. My thoughts roamed more deeply through the dark woods of my mind. Is that what was lurking in the shadows, a sense of anger at Sierra herself for doing this to me, for falling—or jumping—into the pool, for making me so miserable? Was I really angry at her deep inside? Was she the one I needed to forgive?

Thinking back to that August afternoon, I could see Sierra standing by the pool, eating potato chips in her polka-dot bathing suit. I saw her so clearly, it was as if I could touch her smooth skin and kiss her flushed cheek. Through the twirling mists of memory, of reality, of dreams; across the years, the distances, the seas that separated us now, my heart spoke to my little girl: I love you, Sierra, and I'm sorry I wasn't there to save you. I'm not angry at you. I may have been once, but I'm not anymore. I'm just happy I had you to love and cherish for a little while. You can be free now.

A strange feeling suddenly washed over me, and I inhaled the earthy scent of the forest. I looked around at the trees and ferns, the browns and greens of the forest growing dim in the waning light, and suddenly longed to be out of the dark woods under the open sky.

—◆◆◆—

On the Fourth of July, we camped in Rambouillet, France. We cooked hamburgers and hot dogs on the grill and hung a small American flag on our camper. I felt happy to be heading back to America again, finally ready to embrace my own land after turning my back on it.

A Frenchman walked by and wished us, "Good Independence Day." How appropriate, I mused. I did feel independent, ready to face the future rather than hide from it.

Somehow my walk with Leah in the woods seemed to be some kind of breakthrough. The message Leah couldn't fathom had come through to me. "It's not your fault," Sierra was trying to say.

"Don't blame anyone. It just happened, and maybe one day you'll understand why. Just move forward into new landscapes. Look outward. Give to your family, to your friends, to your community. And remember me as you would recall a butterfly that flitted through a few pages of your life, bringing you a certain joy that you will always carry in your heart. Share that joy."

I couldn't explain any of this to anyone. Peter seemed to sense I felt better, and as we explored Versailles one sunny day, he said, "I'm happy to see you smiling so much."

"I'm ready to go back home," I said.

The rain began to fall in Bruges, Belgium. Missy and Emily biked into town and returned drenched and grouchy. Even though it was July, the temperature hovered around sixty degrees, and staying warm and dry became a challenge. We decided to leave Belgium in hopes of finding nicer weather in Maastricht, our next stop.

While the weather was slightly better, it felt weird to be in Maastricht. After showing Missy and Emily the village where we lived, we stopped in to see my old friend, Katharina. She seemed happy to see us, but I felt restless and uncomfortable. The future was calling, and I knew it was time to look forward—not back.

In North Holland, we camped near my in-laws' home in Hoorn, and the rain returned. Peter's mom took ill quite suddenly and was admitted to the hospital, but no one could figure out what was wrong. We said goodbye to Missy and Emily, found a buyer for the Coaster, arranged the container to ship everything back to America, and booked our plane tickets for the end of August. With the camper sold, we were staying in a regular tent, and the rain and wind made conditions miserable.

Peter spent a lot of time at the hospital with his mom, and I was stuck in the campground with three restless boys and nothing to do. I started smoking again. My enthusiasm of a few days before had disappeared completely, and I felt angry and sad and wondered what this year had accomplished. After frittering away tens of thousands of dollars, now we were going right back to the same place we'd started.

What a joke. We had traveled in a huge circle, and it was leading us right back to Virginia. Would everything be the same there? Or would it feel different? Had I changed? Had I learned anything? I tried to summon the feelings I had in the Dordogne, to recall Sierra's message—so clear in Rambouillet, but as I sat smoking in my tent in the rain, all I could feel was sorry for myself again.

I knew what the problem was. I couldn't forgive myself. More than that, there was a sense of self-loathing that dwelled in the belly of my being. It was as if when Sierra died, I stopped loving myself and began instead to despise this terrible person who could let her daughter drown just a few feet away.

That was it. I hated myself. I hated that I let Sierra die. I began to cry in the tent, and the world cried with me, tears falling from the sky. Pounding down from above, the rain seemed to echo my sadness, my anger, my self-pity. The wind blew, and the rain fell, and I tried to make sense of everything: this trip, Sierra, my life, my future, my dreams, my failings. But I couldn't seem to find sense in anything.

Toting an umbrella and wiping my tears, I walked to the activity room at the campground where we were staying and picked up Scott and Jasper. We waited for Peter, who drove up with Ross in the Volvo, our sole means of transportation since we'd loaded the Suburban into the container to be shipped home. We drove through the rain to visit Peter's mother in the hospital.

I was shocked at her appearance. Propped up in the hospital bed, Jannie looked frail and pale and ten years older than the last time I'd seen her. She barely knew who we were, and the kids were frightened to see how old and sick she looked. Peter was overwrought by his mother's mysterious illness, too. It seemed we were falling into a black hole. Again.

Chapter 20

—◦◦◦—

A warm glow within

On the day before we were scheduled to fly back to the States, we paid one last visit to Peter's father and sister. Peter had already said goodbye to his mom, who was still in the hospital. He was finding it hard to leave because his mom wasn't getting better.

"Just go," Karin said. "You can't help by staying here. You need to get back to your lives. I'll take care of things."

As we hugged goodbye, my thoughts wandered to last August, a year ago, when we arrived in the Netherlands. Here we were twelve months later, returning to the place we'd been so anxious to leave, to the home we tried to escape because it didn't feel like home anymore.

What will it feel like now? I wondered.

The next day as we drove to the airport, the kids were strangely quiet. Even Peter seemed lost in thought. I watched the flat Dutch landscape spinning by, the windmills, the quaint farms, and the calm canals that intersected the fields, and thought about the highs and lows of these past weeks: the times I thought I had everything figured out and the times it seemed I was drowning in quicksand, being pulled under by self-doubts and despair. Nothing made sense, and my head hurt from all the thinking.

So I turned my thoughts to Sierra. I remembered how she loved to swing, her laughter rising up higher and higher as she pumped her muscular legs back and forth. "Look at me, Mommy. Look at me," she'd say.

I remembered how she became afraid at the beach once when large waves crashed onto the shore. The tide was rolling in, and Sierra didn't want to sit on the sand anymore, fearful the waves were going to come and take her away.

I remembered how she would pretend to cry when she and Scott got into a tiff. "Boo-hoo-hoo," she'd say, rubbing her eyes with chubby fingers. "Boo-hoo-hoo!" Then she'd peek from behind her hands to see if anyone was paying attention, and if we weren't, she'd cry a little harder: "Boo-hoo-HOO!" Eventually seeing that she wasn't getting any sympathy, she would march resolutely off after her brother to get back that toy or crayon he'd stolen from her.

These memories were all I had left of Sierra. Or were they? I wanted to believe that I'd learned something from this year we'd been away, something that would help me face the future with joy and courage. What I'd found was that there are no simple answers. And, like it or not, it's the highs and the lows, the joy and despair that make life true.

As we turned off the highway and the airport loomed before us, I thought back on our journey and what Sierra's death had taught me about life. I understood now that my family was my home and that even though she wasn't here in the flesh, Sierra was still as much a part of this family as she had been during those two years, nine months, and eight days she lived in our midst. I knew I couldn't hide from her, or she from me. We would always be together.

Our plane took off with a roar through the clear, blue summer sky, heading west. I looked at my sons and my husband and felt a warm glow within. It was Sierra. She was a part of me now, a welcome part. Together we said goodbye to the Old World and prepared to greet the New.

Epilogue

—⟡⟡⟡—

In harmony at last

We burned Sierra's tree one cold winter. It hissed and popped and spit sparks onto my wooden floor, sparks that faded as quickly as they came.

The willow tree we had planted in 1990 in Sierra's memory died a few summers ago. We weren't sure why. It just died all of a sudden. Peter chopped it up for firewood and stacked it in neat piles in the yard. On cold winter nights when the wind blew and the branches shivered, Sierra's tree brought warmth and light into our home.

Soon we would move to a new house a few miles south of the old one. We would pack all of our things into boxes—the photo albums, Peter's coin collection, my goose girl and her little white goose—and we'd say goodbye to this house once more. This time I was sure we wouldn't be coming back.

—⟡⟡⟡—

On a warm winter afternoon, as I stretched in my front yard after an evening run, a huge flock of Canada geese flew overhead. Honking in unison, a hundred or more passed right over me, their V-shaped pattern perfectly symmetrical. As their chorus faded to the east, a hundred more followed in their path, and then a hundred more. I stood in wonder, and as I watched their wings beat against the sky, it seemed for a moment as if they were waving at me. Even after the geese disappeared behind the tall pines across the street, I could hear their cries echoing from afar. I didn't need to see them to know they were there.

—✺✺✺—

A few years ago I hiked into the wildlife refuge where Peter and I had sprinkled Sierra's ashes only to find a chain across the road I needed to take. "Closed," the sign said.

I haven't gone back, but someone told me that section is open again. Maybe it's time to visit the grove of trees once more, to step into the woods, stand beneath the branches, and look down onto the sandy ground.

There, mixed in with pieces of shell, a few fossils, and bits of wood and grass, memories of a young girl's body blend into the earth. In harmony at last.

Photos of Sierra

Christmas 1988: Sierra, 14 months old

Summer 1989: Scott, 3, & Sierra, 21 months

Summer 1989: Peter, Sierra, 21 months old, & Scott, 3, enjoy a ride on the Portsmouth ferry.

Christmas 1989: Sierra, 2

Summer 1990: Scott, Jasper, & Sierra, 2 ½, make mischief in the bathtub.

Summer 1990: On an outing to Portsmouth about a week before Sierra died. This is our last picture of her.

Photos of Europe 1998

March 1998: Feeding the pigeons on St. Mark's Square.

April 1998: Somewhere in Greece

April 1998: Campsite near Athens

April 1998: A beach near Corinth

June 1998: Portugal's craggy cliffs

July 1998: Versailles

About the author

———*∾∾∾*———

Peggy Sijswerda has a B.S. in English from Radford University, an M.A. in English and an M.F.A. in Creative Writing from Old Dominion University. She has written for a variety of regional, national, and international magazines and currently publishes and edits a regional women's magazine called *Tidewater Women* (tidewaterwomen.com). Peggy lives with her family in Virginia Beach.

Please send your comments to sijswerda@hotmail.com and visit www.peggysijswerda.com for more information or to order additional copies of *Still Life with Sierra*.

16530557R00087

Made in the USA
Lexington, KY
30 July 2012